A Matter of Rats

AMITAVA KUMAR

A Matter of Rats

A SHORT BIOGRAPHY OF PATNA

Duke University Press   Durham   2014

Printed in the United States of America on acid-free paper ∞
Designed by Courtney Leigh Baker
Typeset in Whitman by Copperline Book Services, Inc.

Library of Congress Cataloging-in-Publication Data
Kumar, Amitava, 1963–
A matter of rats : a short biography of Patna / Amitava Kumar.
pages cm
Includes bibliographical references and index.
ISBN 978-0-8223-5704-9 (cloth : alk. paper)
1. Patna City (India)—Description and travel.
2. Kumar, Amitava, 1963–
3. Patna City (India)—Biography.
I. Title.
DS486.P26K86 2014
915.4'123—dc23 2013041901

FOR MY PARENTS and FOR RAHUL, who wanted a book about the Power Rangers instead

CONTENTS

ACKNOWLEDGMENTS ix

INTRODUCTION The Place of Place xi

1 The Rat's Guide 1

2 Pataliputra 15

3 Patna in the Hole 29

4 Leftover Patna 45

5 Other Patnas 63

6 Emperor of This World 73

7 Emotional *Atyachaar* 85

EPILOGUE Place of Birth / Place of Death 103

NOTES 109   INDEX 113

ACKNOWLEDGMENTS

This book was written between July 2012 and May 2013. My thanks to the people who spoke to me and the journalists who helped me. The term "emotional *atyachaar*," the title of the last chapter, could be translated as "emotional oppression"; it is borrowed from a song by the same name sung by the fictitious band "Patna ke Presley" in the Hindi hit film *Dev. D*. My thanks to Anurag Kashyap, the filmmaker and my friend, for affirming the swagger of the vernacular. The reader will notice that several statements made in Hindi or Urdu are followed by their English translation, but in a few other places Hindi words have been left untranslated. I didn't think it useful to translate words like *kachori* or *jalebi*, though I would like the reader to eat his or her fill of such Patna delicacies. Where it seemed necessary, names of individuals have been changed.

This is a work of nonfiction. In recent years we have seen an increase in nonfiction writing and sales of books in that genre. There is repeated talk at literary festivals and other venues about the public's hunger for truth. We are told that a reading public—turned off by television propaganda and disenchanted with fiction's flimsy pretensions—is famished for hard realities. I'm exaggerating, of course, but this argument on behalf of incontestable truth is now quite common. I don't agree with it. There is no truth in nonfiction; there is only perspective. In *Rashomon*, Akira Kurosawa's well-known classic, the woodcutter expresses his doubts about two versions of the story to which he was himself a witness. "It's a lie. It's all a lie. Tajomaru's story and the woman's." (Of course, the story that the woodcutter told the court is a lie, too. But that will be discovered later.) The thief listening to the woodcutter says to him: "It's human to lie. Most of the time we can't even be honest with ourselves." An important task of the nonfiction writer is to put down, as accurately as possible, the conditions under which one story is told in place of another. I am grateful to David Davidar for asking me to write this essay, and to Ken Wissoker for enthusiastically supporting the whole project. It gave me the chance to examine the distance that divides different versions of the truth that I, and others, have told about Patna. And also about ourselves.

INTRODUCTION **The Place of Place**

Each book, like a place on a map joined by roads and rivers to other places, is always connected to other books. That is certainly true for this book about my hometown, Patna. There is another facet to this argument: places seemingly unconnected might well be very near each other in terms of literary representation. In my book, New York is closer to Patna than is usually imagined.

When a publisher in Delhi asked me to write about Patna, he mentioned as a possible model E. B. White's classic essay *Here Is New York*.[1] I bought a used copy from a bookstore. The little book had an inscription in blue ink: "Nancy, You may be leaving New York but hopefully New York will never leave you. It has been a pleasure and a delight. Best always, Robert. 06.08.2001." Was he saying that he wished and hoped that she would never forget him? Was the city a giant stand-in for his presence in her life? And what was one to make of the fact that the book had been sold to a second-hand bookstore? I wondered whether the owner, or someone else, had sold it after the September 11 attacks. White's essay had been given a prophetic tone during the aftermath because of the following lines near the end: "The city, for the first time in its long history, is destructible. A single flight of planes no bigger than a wedge of geese can quickly end this island fantasy, burn the towers."[2]

For me, the book's promise lay in the very first sentence of White's foreword: "This piece about New York was written in the summer of 1948 during a hot spell."[3] It gave me hope that if I braved Patna's heat and humidity, I too could put together an essay about a city. Maybe even before the year was out. When the summer ended, I was going to start teaching a writing course, and my new mantra for my students was going to be: "Write every day and walk every day." A hundred and fifty words daily. And a brief round of mindful walking. But producing the small number of words was key. Even if I stuck just to that target, I'd have nearly twenty thousand words before the semester was over. That would be three times the length of White's essay. Roger Angell was White's stepson, and in the edition of the book that I had bought, he had noted that White came down to New York by train, from New England, and took a room at the Algonquin Hotel. After his brief stay, White went back home to Maine and wrote *Here Is New York*. As if it were a secret talisman, I took White's book with me to Patna.

"New York blends the gift of privacy with the excitement of participation." White had written that in a city like New York, people are always insulated from all kinds of events going on around them: "The biggest ocean-going ships on the North Atlantic arrived and departed. I didn't notice them and neither did most other New Yorkers."[4] When I read lines like these, I felt that they expressed a truth not about cities but about writers. Or at least the kind of writer that E. B. White was. He wasn't hunting for headlines. He wasn't even outgoing. He didn't want to be everywhere or, in fact, anywhere.

Unlike White, who had no interest in claiming the role of witness to the Lions' Convention, or the governor's visit, or the death of a man from a falling cornice, I wanted to be a camera with a thousand eyes. Like New York, Patna is a big city and a heavily populated one. But there is a difference. In Patna, an individual like me can never really be removed from the events around him or her, not least because everyone is most likely to be surrounded by family. I didn't desire insulation, but neither did I seek out the chief minister's rally or a Bollywood star's banquet. I wanted only the fullest encounter with the ordinary and, although this became clearer to me later, I was often inclined to search for that which would have engaged me most fully if I were living and working in Patna. Each day I would go out with a Moleskine notebook with its brown paper cover. Here, chosen almost at random, is a log of a single day, August 21, 2012, based on observations I had made that day in my notebook, this one number 18.

9:00 AM. On a visit to Patna railway station to pick up brochures at their tourism booth. Women with bright yellow vests with antipolio slogans. A coolie leading a blind man to his train. Then I see a father holding the hand of a crippled child. And immediately afterward, an old man who manages to walk by himself but his arms and even his torso are propped up by his three sons. His less frail wife lags behind. You want tenderness—a sapling that is to be watered daily—come to the train station.

Just like the old times, the A. H. Wheeler bookstand on Platform 1. And like before, along with treatises by Vivekanand and Nehru, also displayed for sale is Hitler's *Mein Kampf.* I notice that there are now electric outlets for charging mobile phones. Outside, the line of lepers sitting in a line, begging bowls in front of them, just as I remembered from my youth.

10:00 AM. I sit crammed in the back of a Maruti with a journalist and a young cultural activist. The car belongs to a soft-spoken magistrate, who sits in front. The air-conditioning is not working; we are all sweating at the back. The activist belongs to a group called Abhiyan Sanskriti Manch. He tells me he is interested in "cultural studies," and his model is Jacques Rancière's *Proletarian Nights*. I mention to him that I'm supposed to watch a play rehearsal that evening, and he says that Patna is an important center of theater, with twelve to fifteen groups active at any given time.

11:00 AM. Our small party reaches Patna City. The government press in Gulzarbagh is there. This building served as the opium warehouse under the British. The journalist has promised to take me inside, but then we learn that permission is required. We wait in the office of the area's Deputy Superintendent of Police, a man in his thirties, a graduate in English literature from Patna University. He is candid and admits that his degree was of no use to him. He goes on to say that his daughter has been learning about lilies at a local school run by missionaries. She doesn't know what lilies look like. He would prefer that she learn about marigolds.

Noon. Permission has not yet been granted. A fax needs to be sent with a document attesting to my scholarly interest in the press. But then there is a power cut. More time passes while the electric generator is started. The police officer tells me that the best opium is still made in the area, in a nearby town called Raghopur. His district, he says, is the main site of transportation. I have an appointment elsewhere at 3:00 PM, so rather than wait for the bureaucrats to fax the permission letter, I walk over to the press building.

The sun is hot, and out on the dusty street the heat produces a feeling of near suffocation. Any shade is a blessing. On the boundary wall of the press are painted graphic warnings, with prominent yellows and reds, listing the diseases that result from using open areas for passing human waste. In a picture painted alongside, a man with a can looks at the blue door of pink brick toilet. He looks unhappy, perhaps because he is waiting. There is another figure in the picture. He is washing his hands under a tap. He is smiling. Next to this wall poster is another showing a couple with a newborn baby. The man, with a mustache covering his upper lip in such a way that you doubt the lip's existence, is saying something. The man's words are painted below in Hindi. He is saying, "We will give each other another child in another three years." The condom that is being advertised has as its symbol a black stallion standing up on its hind legs.

The press is a large, two-story, white-washed building with wooden doors and borders around the windows painted an earthy red. I see that it is dark and cavernous inside, but don't try to get access. The heat has a way of making you feel dull and opiated.

1:00 PM. I am a few minutes late for class at Patna College. Professor Muniba Sami has allowed me to attend her lecture on Samuel Beckett's *Waiting for Godot*.

3:00 PM. Lunch with Professors Sami and Dutt. *Masala dosa* and *kaathi* roll.

5:00 PM. I stop at the Tricel bookstore and ask Raghu—the owner, whom I have known since my boyhood—what kinds of books do his customers buy these days. He says, without hesitation, *Wings of Fire*, the autobiography of the former President of India, Abdul Kalam. In Raghu's shop there are children's books on the floor; a separate shelf of scholarly titles from Oxford; two shelves with Penguin India titles; a shelf devoted to Hindi literature; and on the opposite side, in a riot of blood, lust, and loathing, titles by John Grisham, Robert Ludlum, and Ayn Rand.

6:00 PM. The traffic constables are women, and yes, I see this as empowerment. We pass a small restaurant called Subah Ka Nashta. The menu is painted under the name (6 puris, 2 *jalebis*, Price: 23 rupees). It doesn't get less crowded away from the railway station. In a few minutes, the car creeps up to Exhibition Road. We move so slowly it gives me time to look out and search for the hardware shop owned by a friend who was in school with me. I haven't seen him since that time, decades ago, when his father was knifed in a hotel room by a boy he had brought up since childhood. I had imagined a bull in a small courtyard, bleeding from a thousand cuts. I don't find the shop but, after some difficulty, am able to locate the building where the rehearsal is taking place. There are no lights on the ground floor. I'm told to go a floor up for the elevator. A small red glowing button in the dark to tell me that I'm in the right place. Then, in the near total darkness, the elevator appears and the doors part. A thin old man sitting on a stool inside asks, "Which floor?"

On the seventh floor, members of the Patna branch of Indian People's Theatre Association (IPTA) are rehearsing a Girish Karnad play. The original was in Kannada, but the Hindi version is called *Rakt-Kalyan*. Shoes have been left outside. On one of the walls, framed portraits of Bhagat Singh and the poet Kaifi Azmi. Red plastic chairs are arranged in a large rectangle in the room. The actors sit with the script in their hands. The play is about Brahmins and the revolt against caste. While the actors read out their lines, I study the dirty soles of their feet.

Most of the actors are young. But the older ones, three men and two women, are experienced theater activists. When they speak their lines, time seems to slow down. There is enough time for meaning to take shape and even grow. One of the older actors plays a Brahmin who has renounced all trappings of caste. He is impressive. But so is the actor who plays the low-born king. The play is set in the twelfth century but it has great relevance for Patna, where caste is the currency of social exchange. The king has a crude, candid manner—it makes me think of Lalu Yadav—and he tells his interlocutor that his low birth is branded on his forehead: "You ask the most innocent child in my empire: what is Bijjala by caste? And the instant reply will be: a barber! One's caste is like the skin on one's body. You can peel it off top to toe, but when the new skin forms, there you are again: a barber—a shepherd—a scavenger!"

10:00 PM. My sisters are talking in the room that is at the far end of the house. This used to be my room when I was a boy. I'm downloading photographs on my computer, but I eavesdrop on their conversation. My elder sister is a doctor, married to a doctor. He has a sister, who is a doctor—and her husband, also a doctor, is having an affair. The woman with whom he is having the affair is not a doctor. She is the receptionist at his hospital. They meet for sex at a gym that is across the street from the hospital.

THE CITY IS HOME to a multitude of facts. And yet, how ordinary is the ordinary? In the public imagination, in India at least, Patna is an open city. It has surrendered to the might of scandalous stories. Kidnappings! Corruption! Crime! Here is a case that was a favorite of mine for several years. The journalist Arvind Das wrote in *The Republic of Bihar* about a conversation overheard in a train from Patna in 1991: A woman, distraught at her husband's prolonged illness, was telling her son that she sometimes found herself wanting to commit suicide. The son responded that his father's death would be more welcome. Das had written, "Why should you die, why not kill *Babuji* instead? If he goes away, we will get his gratuity and provident fund money and it is possible that I might even get a job on compassionate grounds. What use will your dying be?" Das noted in his book that the boy was only twelve years old.[5]

And yet, as often happens in Bihar, the state of which Patna is the capital, it is also possible to tell the opposite story. Das features in this one too. In Delhi, during a visit last summer, I went for a walk in the garden around Humayun's tomb. My companion was the esteemed social thinker Ashis Nandy. We were talking about Bihar, and Nandy said that there were many news reports back in the 1990s about young Bihari men being forced to marry at gunpoint. In most cases, a youth traveling in a train would find himself looking up into the barrel of a gun. He would be asked to disembark and would be taken to a town or a village where he would be married to a girl whose family had guns but not the means to pay an expensive dowry. Nandy told me that he had asked Das, who was from a village only a couple of hours away from Patna, whether there wasn't a lot of fear on the part of the bride's family that their daughter would be abandoned or killed? Das had said to him: "But that too is Bihar! So far I have not heard about a single such case where the young woman has been harmed."

But that too is Bihar! When Nandy finished telling me his story, I thought of a line from John Berger's Booker Prize–winning novel, *G.*: "Never again will a single story be told as though it were the only one."[6] It could be a credo for nonfiction writers. To show on the page that despite what you're saying, there is another story waiting in the wings. The ordinary kept from being made extraordinary—the tame fascination with the exotic—because it is never removed from the context of surrounding facts. Rats are to be found in my parents' home in Patna, yes, but they become real to me, as I sit listening to them at night, because of the research done on rats in New York City.[7]

"It was years before I saw that the most important thing about travel, for the writer, was the people he found himself among." This was V. S. Naipaul writing in *Beyond Belief*, an account of his travels in Indonesia, Iran, Pakistan, and Malaysia.[8] What Naipaul was saying about travel to foreign countries is also true for the writer who is only returning home. This long essay is about my hometown, Patna, but at its heart are stories about people. People, not political programs. "Has Patna improved?" Questions of this nature are often directed at those who know Patna. I have little interest in answering such questions. The emphasis on the ordinary means that my attempt here has been to present stories of daily lives. My themes here are similar to what I would have explored if I were writing about people elsewhere: success, failure, love, death. I have written earlier that there are no people in postcolonial theory. Almost the same can be said about place. A term like "postcolonial" swallows up whole continents and nations. This book is about a particular place called Patna, and I cannot deny that my portrait is personal. In this, too, I'm reaching for the ordinary, paying attention to what remains obscure and whose value is overlooked. In the last paragraph of *Here Is New York*, E. B. White wrote about an old, battered willow tree in the city. He wanted the tree saved. White hadn't ignored the vision of the tall towers and the terrible errands of the flying planes, but what mattered was the tree: "If it were to go, all would go."[9] In the pages of this book that I have written about Patna, I too have something that I want to save. I have in mind two residents of Patna who have spent a lifetime there. They have survived the city's troubles and celebrated its achievements, and they will not be around forever. Patna is the place where I grew up, but those two are my real place of origin. And when they are gone, my link to Patna will be broken.

One final prefatory remark. The place of place is also in writing. In other words, a writer arrives at a sense of place not by mere accident of birth or habitation but by creating, again and again, a landscape of the imagination. I'm flooded with memories of my past grant applications: "Dear Sir/Madam, I am writing to apply for funds to travel to Patna to conduct research in areas of peasant unrest. My primary interest is in the cultural production of protest." Articles, travel pieces, memoirs. A practice carried out over years of return, akin to a pattern of writing and revision. In a changing city, the urgent need to record my deepest associations. Even in fiction, the desire to put down precisely the arrival of the monsoon in Patna:

> Rains lashed the house, driving water inside through the cracks in the windows, making the wooden window frames swollen and gray. The ceiling in the bathroom turned green and began to drip. If the front door was left open in the evening, frogs hopped in and took their place on the floor around the sofa, looking

very much like well-fed but malcontent guests. The pages of the notebooks reserved for homework got stuck together and could only with some ingenuity be used to make paper boats. Binod and Rabinder would return from school with their hair damp and their clothes soiled with mud. Wet garments were spread to dry on every available piece of furniture and also under the sluggishly turning blades of the ceiling fans. There was a clothesline even in the kitchen. Most of the walls became furred with peeling paint and centipedes of different colors crawled on them and found their way onto beds and pillows. It suddenly seemed during those months that there was very little space in the house for its real inhabitants.[10]

The mere act of typing these words, copying them from the page open in front of me, provides an entry into that place of writing. The location of culture is not so much a place but an active practice—the practice of writing.

THE LATEST STEP I took in that place of place, immediately before beginning this book, was writing a short piece for the India Ink blog for the *New York Times*.[11] I had just read *Jeff, One Lonely Guy*, by Jeff Ragsdale, David Shields, and Michael Logan. Ragsdale, a New York writer and unemployed comedian, had reacted to a breakup by posting flyers near his home that simply said: "If anyone wants to talk about anything, call me. (347) 469-3173. Jeff, one lonely guy."[12]

Jeff, One Lonely Guy was fashioned out of the 60,000 calls and text messages that Ragsdale received in response to his flyers. The responses were varied and fascinating:

"I called to see what the story was."

"We live in a disconnected society. Did you think up this idea while you were smoking a blunt?"

"I just flew in from L.A. and was in a bad mood, then I saw your sign on the street. Ha! I cast reality shows."

"Heathcliff it's me Catherine!"

"Pablo Escobar had a hit out on my father, who was a Communist. My father fought against Escobar and got political asylum in the U.S."[13]

All this in the first handful of pages. The writer David Shields, who was one of Ragsdale's teachers, helped edit these field notes from that occult zone Shields calls "Occupy Loneliness."

In my piece for the *Times* I proposed that I could put up flyers on the busy streets near my parents' home asking questions like "Does the best opium still come from Patna?" In one of my writing notebooks is a picture I had torn out from a glossy magazine several years ago. I was in a gym in Florida, and the page left open on a treadmill showed a nineteenth-century drawing of swarthy, dhoti-clad men at work in an immense hall, arranging in neat lines circular mounds of—what?

The text above the picture offered a clue: "Connoisseurs, he says, argue as to the source of the finest opium. Some say the best opium comes from Patna, India, along the southern bank of the Ganges." My flyer would be an attempt to find out if that was still true.

I also had other questions.

In 1967 there was a famine in Bihar. I knew of this only because my father, a career bureaucrat, served in places like Purnea, a city to the east of Patna. But then I discovered a newsreel, in which I saw the actor Marlon Brando listening to villagers near Patna. I learned that Brando had come to Bihar as the ambassador for the United Nations Children's Fund. You can hear voices in the background, complaining in Hindi of hunger and of grain being denied to them by corrupt officials.

And then the Englishman providing the voice-over says, "All in all, it was a modest performance from Brando, and definitely a non-speaking part."

So that could be another flyer: "Did you see Brando in Patna in 1967?"

I never posted flyers, but this book is made up in part by the answers I received in response to the questions like the one above. It bears mentioning that a man who had met Brando in 1967 in Bihar was not in Patna but in upstate New York. He was an American engaged in famine relief in India in the 1960s.

Objects in the mirror are closer than they appear. In the mirror of literature representation, places find a new intimacy, not only to us but also to each other. Nonetheless, what the above record doesn't reveal is the writer's anxiety. What does it matter that Patna and New York are connected? When I was waiting to hear news about the novel that I have quoted from above, news about whether it had been accepted for publication in the United States, a friend from Patna—a fellow writer—expressed his feelings of impatience in a letter: "I truly believe that getting published in the West is not that important. At best it is a bonus and one earns more, which is a good thing. But as Indian writers, our primary market lies here and it is here in India that we will be finally judged, though I do realize that some critics here do look towards publication in the West as final validation of a writer's worth. But tell me, is Paul Auster ever bothered about how he is perceived in India? Or whether his books sell at all in India?" I don't know; I have no idea whether he has heard of Patna. But in the pages that follow, I have written of Patna in the belief that Patna would be of interest to anyone, particularly Paul Auster.

Rats have burrowed under the railway tracks in Patna. I imagine the rats, as citizens of a literal underworld, inhabiting a spreading web of small safe houses and getaway streets. We could choose to call it a city under the city, but if that is too sophisticated a description for at least one of the two entities, then let's just call it a dense warren of subterranean burrows. In places, the railway platform has collapsed. In my mind's eye, I watch a train approaching Patna Junction in the early morning. The traveler sees the men sitting beside the tracks with their bottoms exposed, plastic bottles of water on the ground in front of them, often a mobile phone pressed to the ear. But at night the first inhabitants of Patna that the visitor passes are the invisible ones: warm, humble, highly sociable, clever, fiercely diligent rats.

In the library at Patna University, I heard that rats had taken over a section of the stacks and the library had been closed. Also, there are rats—always, in these stories, rats as big as cats—in the Beur Jail. After he was shifted there from an air-conditioned clubhouse that had served as a makeshift prison, the jail was home for a while to the former chief minister of Bihar, Lalu Prasad Yadav. He tended a vegetable garden in prison and issued orders to visiting politicians and bureaucrats. Another inmate of Beur Jail is a former legislator, Pappu Yadav, who is on trial for the murder of a communist leader but has been awarded degrees in human rights and disaster management while behind bars. But I digress.

For some reason, even in the Patna Museum—home to Mauryan art and Buddhist relics, including, some say, the ashes of Lord Buddha—there are stuffed rats nailed to black wooden bases. About fifty feet away stands the magnificent, glistening third century BCE sculpture of the Didarganj Yakshi. A long and heavy necklace dangles in the gap between her globular stone breasts. In her right hand, she holds a fly whisk flung languidly over her shoulder. And running away from her are the stuffed rats, a small procession of them, rotting and seemingly blinded with age, breathing the air of eternity under dusty glass.

Outside in the city, however, and—one can be certain—in other parts of the museum, the rats are alive and dangerous. Newspapers periodically carry reports that babies have been bitten by rats. One such report helpfully explained that it was the traces of food on the unwashed faces of infants that attracted the rodents. Rats are curious, especially about food, and they will eat anything. In the hospital in Patna where my sister works, nurses play the radio at night because they are firmly of the belief that the music keeps the rats from nibbling at their toes.

In the middle of the night one winter, during a visit to Patna, I was sitting at the dining table with my jet-lagged two-year-old son, watching a cartoon on my computer. I had turned on only a single, dim light as I didn't want my parents to be disturbed. We must have been sitting there quietly for about half an hour before my little boy asked, "Baba, what is that?" He was pointing beyond the screen. There were two enormous rats walking away from us. They looked like stout ladies on tiny heels, on their way to the market. I wouldn't have been surprised to see them carrying small, elegant handbags.

The next morning, when my son told my wife about the rats he had seen—he was first confused and said that they were rabbits—she was alarmed. But no one else was. Despite how ubiquitous the rats were in Patna, or perhaps because they were ubiquitous, no one seemed to pay much attention to them. I would bring them up in conversation, and people would laugh and launch into stories about them. One person told me that the Patna police had claimed that rats were drinking from the bottles of illegal liquor seized by the authorities and stored in warehouses. I didn't believe the story—I said that I smelled a rat—and so a link was duly sent to me. In the press report, a senior police officer named Kundan Krishnan was quoted as saying: "We are fed up with these drunken rats and cannot explain why they have suddenly turned to consumption of alcohol."[1]

For a while I had hoped to get a professional pest control agency to come and trap rats in the house in Patna. The problem was a pressing one—rats had carried away my mother's dentures. But all I could find was a man who would come and put packets of rat poison in different rooms. People suggested that I buy traps and put food inside; the same people admitted that the rats were too smart to get caught in such traps. I detected a note of pride in such statements. My sister told me that her hospital had bought an expensive piece of ultrasonic machinery that emitted a high-frequency sound to keep rats away. The sound was inaudible to human ears, and my sister said that things were okay for a while. Then they noticed that a rat had bitten through the electric cord. Since then, the machine had simply stood unused in a corner.

We were visiting Patna from upstate New York. Just a month earlier, *New York* magazine had run a feature on rats, calling them "one of evolution's more triumphant guilty pleasures."[2] Rats are one of New York City's obsessions. They are neither as invincible as bed bugs nor as common as cockroaches, but they make for more scary YouTube videos. Of course, no trip to the waterfront goes unrewarded by a rat sighting, and they are a constant feature of the city's subways and sewers. During those nights in Patna, when I lay awake in bed listening to the movement of rats in the dark, odd details from the *New York* article would come to me. Rats can get pregnant within eighteen hours of having given birth, and they can produce a litter twenty-one days after impregnation. They can swim for more than half a mile, tread water for three days, and, my mother claims, sometimes even emerge through the toilet bowl. They can gnaw through concrete and collapse their skeletons to fit through a hole no bigger than a quarter. Rats can also go two weeks without sleeping.

I didn't find an exterminator in Patna. But I did meet a man who wanted rats to be killed for food. Vijoy Prakash is a senior official in the Bihar administration—the principal secretary in the Department of Rural Development—and he has caused controversy by suggesting that restaurants should put rat meat on their menus. Questions about this proposal were raised in the Bihar legislature, and the papers had reported on it with some relish. I met Prakash in his office in the Old Secretariat in Patna. He was a kind-looking man, quiet and dark skinned, his eyebrows flecked with gray. In a spacious, air-conditioned office, Prakash was working on a report at his desk. I looked around while I waited. A wooden board to my right listed the names of the administrators who had served in that office. The names were carefully painted in white on the varnished wood. Number 22 on that list, the last name, was Prakash's. I noted with pleasure and surprise that number 7 was my father. My father, who retired from service long ago, must have occupied the chair on which Prakash was now sitting, when I was still a student. Had I ever visited my father in this room, bringing him lunch during a trip home? I couldn't remember if I had.

Prakash, who studied astrophysics, is a rationalist. He wants people to have more enlightened views about nature and society. His mission, I realized when we began talking, isn't simply to change the popular perception of rats. Instead, it is to alter the views that most people have of a particular community near the bottom of the social ladder: the Musahars, known all over Bihar as the rat-eating caste. Prakash says that rats trapped in fields have long been a part of the Musahars' diet, and there is no reason why others cannot also benefit from protein-rich rat meat. His main point was to engineer change in the living conditions of the Musahars, who are among the poorest and most marginalized groups in Bihar. If rats were accepted as a popular food item, and as a consequence rat farming was commercialized, the Musahars' income would inevitably go up. Like every good bureaucrat I've met, Prakash rattled off statistics to support his theory. In 1961 the rate of literacy among Musahars was merely 2.5 percent; forty years later, the rate of literacy had risen to only 9 percent. As far as rats were concerned, in a country and state where a significant percentage of people went hungry, rats ate 30–40 percent of the crops. In each rat hole excavated in a field, you could find up to fourteen kilograms of grain. When these two facts are appraised side by side, Prakash pointed out, his plan makes even more sense.

I wasn't entirely convinced, but Prakash was unfazed by my skepticism. He said that even as recently as fifty years ago, chicken wasn't allowed in many homes in Patna. It was just a matter of time before rats would be "domesticated" and eaten in homes.

"Have you eaten a rat?" I asked.

"Yes," he said, in the Musahar *toli* in Naubatpur. He had gone there with his wife, a teacher, and they had been invited to have lunch with the family they were visiting. The rats had been fried and then cooked in a curry. The dish was served with rice and tasted delicious.

I had known Musahar families in my village in Champaran. In fact, once when I was a boy, I had just finished bathing at the hand pump a little distance from my grandmother's house when a woman approached me. Behind her was a child wearing a ragged pair of shorts. He was younger than me, maybe seven or eight years old. I remember very clearly that the woman was tall, with curly hair, and her sari was mustard colored. She asked me politely when I was going to return to Patna. My father had said we were to leave in an hour.

"Can't you take him with you?"

I had seen the woman before in the village. I don't think I had spoken to her. The boy was trying to hide behind his mother. The woman spoke again because I had said nothing.

"He will play with you. He will do all the work that needs to be done in the house. Take him with you. There is not enough here for him to eat."

I went back to the house and pointed out the woman to my mother or an aunt. Somebody recognized her. I was told that she was a Musahar. She wanted her son to be a servant in our home in Patna. We were upper caste, and I was told that my grandmother would not allow a Musahar to step inside the house.

MANY YEARS WOULD PASS before I would read Phanishwar Nath Renu's memoir about doing relief work during the flood caused by the waters of the Mahananda in 1949.[3] Kerosene was needed, and matches, and medicine for feet that were rotting from prolonged exposure to water. Renu, along with a doctor, traveled through the flood-hit areas in a boat. He wrote that they had heard that for several days the Musahars had been eating any fish and rats that they had managed to singe over a fire. Once the two of them reached the flooded *basti*, they heard the sound of the *dhol* and cymbals. A platform had been erected over the water and served as a stage. A dance was in progress. Wearing a red sari, a dark-skinned Musahar man was pretending to be a bride; behind the figure in the sari was the husband, begging her to come back home. But the bride refused, complaining about her abusive mother-in-law and her sister-in-law's sharp tongue. It was now the husband's turn to sing a song. He promised to break his sister's legs and to push his mother out of the house. The audience, smeared with mud and hungry, was full of laughter. In the course of writing this book, like the great writer Renu, I would sometimes find joy among those I had expected only to be burdened by pathos. Joy is less common, no doubt, but is as real as suffering. Writers often demonstrate inordinate zeal when portraying the misery of the downtrodden and the oppressed: it is only a form of narcissism with the writer enamored of his or her sensitive self faithfully recording the pain of others. No doubt I am guilty of this, too, but I plead equal fondness for folly, pleasure, guile, greed, and hypocrisy. Hence the rats.

The day after I met Vijoy Prakash in his office in Patna, I went with my father to our village. The journey used to take several hours, but I was told that it now took half the time to reach our destination because of a new bypass that had been built in order to promote tourism to nearby Buddhist sites like the stupa near Kesaria. (This is a Bihar specialty. No one tells you the distance between two places in miles; instead, because everything depends on the condition of the roads, space is always discussed in terms of time.) Of course, there were delays. A long line of trucks idled on the side of the road. The highway had been blocked by angry youth demonstrating because of the death of a man injured in an accident. The victim had been taken to a nearby government hospital, but as no doctor had shown up for work for several days, the man succumbed to his injuries. The protestors had made a truck driver park his vehicle across the road and, for good measure, also put a log and broken furniture in the path of approaching vehicles. We had no option but to turn back. For a while, even this was not allowed. I first showed sympathy to the gathered youth, but then I took out my press pass and threatened them with severe consequences if we were not allowed on our way. They relented after a while, and we took narrow rural roads around the blockage and reemerged onto the highway after about half an hour.

I was returning to my ancestral home for the first time since my grandmother's death more than a decade ago. On the small platform with the *tulsi* plant, where my grandmother had poured water each morning, someone had put fresh hibiscus. But other than that small touch, a look of decay pervaded the house. I walked through the empty corridors and looked at the locked doors of the uninhabited rooms where I had spent all my holidays. A feeling of great melancholy washed over me. Suddenly, alone in an empty corridor, I began to weep. I missed my grandmother's voice, or maybe only my childhood. In any case, I didn't linger. I had come here on a small anthropological mission, not to surrender to nostalgia. I wanted a Musahar to show me how he caught a rat.

Sinhasan, a mild-mannered, middle-aged man I remembered from the past, was working on the construction of a hospital near our ancestral house that our family was funding. It would be named after my grandmother. My father had made the journey to check on how work on the project was going. Sinhasan, a Musahar, didn't want to put me to any trouble. He said I could sit in the shade; he would go into the fields, catch the rats, and bring them to me.

"No," I said, "you don't understand. I want to observe how you catch them."

He called out to two other men, also Musahars, and we started walking to the fields. One of the men was carrying a *kudaal* for digging. The monsoon rains had left the ground soft and wet. My shoes sank into the mud. Sinhasan said that it was very easy to catch rats before the rains, early in the summer, when the wheat had ripened and was still standing in the fields.

"Rats make holes and save a lot of grain for their young. They are hopping around at that time, and we catch them and cook them right here."

"How do they taste?" I asked.

"Good," he said.

"Is it like chicken?"

Sinhasan paused for a second and then said, "*Murgi se zyaada tayyar hai.*" It is better than chicken.

At the edge of a field, where it was drier, the men stopped. They had seen a little mound of freshly dug earth. The man with the *kudaal* was named Phuldeo. He showed me a few scattered grains lying underfoot, evidence of a rat nearby, and then he began to dig. The day was so hot and humid that within a minute or two sweat was dripping off his nose and chin. The little trench he was digging was about two feet wide, and by the time he had finished it was four feet in length. I saw that Sinhasan and the third man, whose name was Chapraasi, had positioned themselves on either side of the trench. Both men were around forty, with thin, sinewy limbs. They looked sturdy but had both adopted such a relaxed stance that I got a bit worried. When I asked if the rat wouldn't get away, Sinhasan smiled and brushed aside my question.

Phuldeo said he could see the rat hole. Two more heaves, and he bent down. The rat's snout was visible to him. A quick flick of his hand, and he had caught it. Phuldeo held the rat up, and I saw its lower incisors, which were long and curved. They were a dirty yellow, the color of old toenails. Sinhasan said: "If it doesn't cut with those teeth night and day, those teeth will go right through its head. It can eat through brick. Even when it's sleeping, its mouth keeps moving."

I said that I wanted to take a picture and in that moment, while Phuldeo tried to give me a better view of the rat's head, it bit him on the finger. Blood spurted out. I took pictures of the tiny ears, the luxuriant hairs around its nose, and—above those dirty yellow teeth—the glinting black eyes.

We let the rat return to the field. My Musahar informants told me that in the right season they ate rats about three or four times a week. Four or five of them were enough for a meal. How did they cook the meat? Over a small fire, the hair was first burned off the body; a small incision was then made in the belly to remove the entrails; following this, spices were rubbed into the meat, and it was fried. I had one last question to put to Sinhasan. A senior bureaucrat in Patna had said to me that people were judged by what they ate. The reason Musahars were looked down on in Bihar was that they ate rats. The official believed that if we all began to think about rats in a more positive way, caste itself would disappear and we would no longer think of Musahars as a lower caste. Did this make sense to them? Did they share the official's optimism?

Sinhasan didn't have to consider this question too long. He said, "Only if everyone else is already of the same view as the official. Then, yes, people's sense of caste will change. Otherwise, no."

Sinhasan was being polite. He was taking care not to throw the question back in my face. High-minded abstractions weren't among his pressing concerns. His worry was finding food for that day and the next. In another five minutes he was going to return to work, mixing cement to build the front brick wall of the hospital. For the day's labor he was going to be paid one hundred and fifty rupees. A generation ago there would have been work only on the landlord's fields, and now there were other kinds, mostly in small industries, and payment in cash. But the conditions of work, and even its availability, were dismal. For those on the bottom of the social ladder, there was only harsh physical labor. The two other men, balanced on bamboo beams behind Sinhasan, flinging water on the bricks and then cementing them, were also Dalits. In the distance, on the patio of my old ancestral home, upper-caste men were sitting on cots. They were poor too, eking out a living as farmers, but none of them was ever likely to do the work that Sinhasan did. One of them, wearing a *lungi*, his bare feet cracked, had followed me out to where I was talking to Sinhasan. This man told me that he had eaten roasted rats when he was a boy playing in the fields. Age had brought him an awareness of his social status, and he had stopped going near rats. He knew the consequences of breaking taboos: "*Shikaayat ho jaayi.*" People would complain.

We drove back to Patna. Once again, there was a delay. Traffic was stalled on the highway: a speeding bus had knocked down a motorcyclist. A red motorcycle lay crushed under its wheel. A part of the tarmac was wet. Was it blood—or oil from the bike? I didn't get out of the car to find out. A fire had been lit in the middle of the road. Once again, I needed to show my press pass to get by.

We were on the highway to progress. It was littered with fresh carnage. This cliché appeared in my mind even before we had left the scene of the accident. Change was visible everywhere. Even our village had changed. The small stores where I once used to buy small packets of Glucose biscuits were now selling mobile phones. The real changes were less visible. Nearly twenty women in the village earned money from the government, working on child development programs. Political and financial power was no longer limited to the upper caste. A few backward-caste families had prospered: my grandfather had once been *mukhiya*, but sometime in my teens the village had elected a new headman, a man from a lower caste. In the last election, because of the implementation of reservation policy—that is, reserving a certain number of offices for people of lower caste—the village barber was elected *mukhiya*. This was an improvement, even if the ideological gains exceeded the material ones and left far too many people behind. The most impoverished group, the Dalits, had improved their lot, but not by very much. The Musahars of my childhood had over the last decade made their way out of bondage to the land. Men like Phuldeo also worked as laborers in Punjab and Andhra, riding on trucks to other parts of the country, but they owned next to nothing. At the same time, the world outside had changed. The village appeared only a stone's throw away from the world of television broadcasting stations and even beauty parlors. A pukka road, shaded by newly planted trees, now connected the village to the nearby town. The villagers didn't even need to make a journey to Patna, which had been the main city when I was young; now they boarded trains that took them directly to Mumbai and Hyderabad. The Bihar of my childhood was now gone, replaced by something entirely new.

FOR A LONG TIME I carried in my mind a Dickensian picture of a cramped space alive with the movement of rats in the dark, one borrowed from the past. In that black-and-white picture, I am ten. My father has gone away to attend a wedding in a village far from Patna. I'm awoken at night by a screeching sound. The sound is unfamiliar; after putting on the light and looking around, I go back to sleep. In the darkness, the screeching resumes. It is only then that— suddenly wide awake—I remember the pet parrot I had been given as a present that very day. The small bamboo cage is no longer on the window ledge where I had placed it before going to sleep. I first spot the green feathers on the floor and then find the bird under my bed. Rats have gnawed through the thin wooden cage and bitten off the parrot's wing. The bird dies the next morning.

Decades later, I put the scene in a novel I wrote about Patna. Crucially, the fictional version had the protagonist's cousin killing rats with a hockey stick. Such dreams of revenge! I think I've been unfair to rats. Are they the pure embodiment of pestilential evil? I'm not sure. When I ask students in my nonfiction classes to write about the environment, they often automatically produce portraits in which nature is separate from the city, remote, gloriously removed from the intimacy of one's bed or bathroom or garbage can. In Patna the rat is an intimate enemy. Rats and humans share Patna's spaces, getting into each other's way; they compete with each other and, in more ways than one, they also kill each other.

Massacre with a hockey stick! There is another way to understand the anger of my revenge: I have some admiration for the rat that, unlike me, hasn't fled Patna and has found it possible to live and thrive there.

Oh, *biradar*, who is the rat now?

CHAPTER TWO **Pataliputra**

I would not have turned to writing if I had been able to draw. When I was thirteen or fourteen and attending school in Patna, I had not yet given up my ambition to become an artist. My earliest models were rulers and saints from our past. The teacher would be delivering his dull lecture on ancient Indian history, and I would try to copy, over and over again, the illustration printed in the textbook.

The Buddha posed a difficulty. The illustration in the book must have been based on a statue in the Gandhara style. His shapely eyes, shut in serene meditation, were the easiest to outline, and above them, the long arched eyebrows in flight; ditto for the full, feminine lips. The trouble began with the intricate, knotted rings of hair; and, it was altogether impossible to draw the perfect circle of the halo around his head.

Pataliputra, which later became Patna, was mentioned very early in that textbook, certainly by page twenty. The city was founded in the sixth century BCE by Ajatshatru, a monarch who was probably a regicide and a patricide. Until he built the fort city at the confluence of the Ganga and Sone Rivers, it was just a village named Pataligram. Gautama Buddha visited Pataligram shortly before his death and, if guidebooks are to be believed, prophesied that a great city would rise there.

Chandragupta Maurya and then Ashoka the Great ruled from Pataliputra. Did I draw them in my notebook, too? I don't recall. I remember learning about Megasthenes, the Greek ambassador to the Mauryan court: he had written that the palaces in Pataliputra were more beautiful than the palaces of Susa and Ecbatana, in ancient Persia. In K. K. Datta's history of Bihar,[1] I read that Megasthenes had described a city oblong in shape, nine and a half miles long and just over a mile wide. It was defended by a moat and a massive timber palisade furnished with sixty-four gates and 570 towers. But all this is academic knowledge. What I remember most vividly about Megasthenes from my boyhood is the claim, perhaps apocryphal, that in Pataliputra people left their doors unlocked.

Those were the days! More than a decade ago, sitting in a room in Brooklyn, when I began to write for the first time about Patna, the words of the Greek ambassador came back to me. In my notebook I wrote: "Those were the days. But they were never there, those days. Or even if they were, they existed only in the pages of the history books."

When Megasthenes wrote in his diary in 303 BCE about people leaving their doors unlocked, I wondered if he could have ever imagined the reality of present-day Patna, where my mother cannot leave her doors unlocked.

Pataliputra's ancient glory is buried in history, but in Kumhrar at the edge of Patna are the sunken remains of a huge Mauryan hall that was once supported by eighty sandstone pillars. Chandragupta Maurya was born in Pataliputra and established India's first empire. He was called Sandracottus or Andracottus by the Greeks, and Plutarch writes that "Andracottus was only a stripling when he met Alexander." He was barely in his twenties when he defeated Alexander's army; his rule extended from the Bay of Bengal in the east to beyond the Indus River in the west. Chandragupta was helped in his conquests by his advisor Chanakya, the author of *Arthashastra* and forever condemned to being called "the Indian Machiavelli" even though he predated the Italian by about 1,800 years. Before his death from starvation, as prescribed by Jain edicts, Chandragupta had led his army—reported by Pliny to consist of 600,000 infantry, 30,000 cavalry, and 9,000 elephants—to triumph over kingdoms south of the Vindhyas and across the Deccan Plateau. The Mauryan rulers, writes the historian Romila Thapar, "gave expression to an imperial vision which was to dominate succeeding centuries of Indian political life."[2]

Perhaps unique among my country's most iconic cities, Patna has had glories only in the distant past. Besides its position of prominence as the capital of some of the greatest monarchs of Indian history such as Chandragupta Maurya and Ashoka, it was also where the Gupta kings reigned during what was called the Golden Age of India (320–550 CE). (I was conscious, while learning about the Gupta Empire, that there was a boy in my class with the surname Gupta. He was short, with oily hair, and, if I remember right, his family owned a local business in bathroom tiles.) The founder of the Gupta dynasty, Chandragupta I (320–335 CE)—what did I know about him? Or, for that matter, about Chandragupta II (380–415 CE), who was distinguished from Chandragupta I by his promotion of the arts? Very little, and what was worse, as a schoolboy I confused both with Chandragupta Maurya. Later I discovered that I wasn't alone in doing this. When I interviewed the former chief minister of Bihar, Lalu Prasad Yadav, about a decade ago, he did the same thing. His wife, Rabri Devi, was chief minister at that time, and the three of us sat outside their home, sipping lemon tea. Lalu was giving me a brief history lesson on the importance of our city. He said piously, "*Itihaas padhne ki zaroorat hai*" (it is necessary to read history). He recited the familiar names from Patna's history. Rather pointedly, he said: "It was here that we had Chandragupta II. His reign is called the Golden Period in Indian history. Chandragupta II was a *shudra*. Ask the historians." I did. The historians clarified that the ruler Lalu had in mind was Chandragupta Maurya—who, it is speculated, was the illegitimate son of a Nanda ruler and a palace maid. Clearly, what was more significant in Lalu's mind, and what he wanted to convey to me in passing, was that Bihar had been ruled by a person who had been born low.

But let us also give Chandragupta II his due. During his reign, toward the end of the fourth century, a Chinese monk named Fa Hien came to Pataliputra on his way to see Buddhist shrines. (Looking now at what Fa Hien wrote about his visit, I discover in a footnote in his book, *A Record of Buddhistic Kingdoms*, the following piece of information: "The modern Patna, lat. 25° 28' N., lon. 85° 15' E. The Sanskrit name means 'The city of flowers.' It is the Indian Florence.")[3] Fa Hien described a kingdom where prosperity reigned and the elements of the modern welfare state appeared to be already in place, particularly in the matter of caring for the sick.

Another notable Chinese monk, Hiuen Tsang, is also associated with Pataliputra. Hiuen Tsang came to India in the second half of the seventh century CE. Portraits of him show a man carrying on his back a strange and elaborate apparatus—it appears to be an enormous cane backpack, curving like a staircase; attached to it is an umbrella that, in turn, has dangling from it a small lamp. Hiuen Tsang spent fifteen years in India, six of them close to Pataliputra, at the university at Nalanda. One of the first great universities in recorded history, Nalanda housed ten thousand students and two thousand faculty members, all drawn from a variety of nations. An initiative has recently been undertaken to revive the university at Nalanda, after a gap of eight hundred years. The Nobel laureate Amartya Sen is among those leading the effort; faculty members from a variety of East Asian nations have promised their support.

About 450 acres of land close to the ruins of the old university have already been earmarked for the site on which the twenty-first-century Nalanda University will be built. On the institution's website are calls for bids from interested security agencies as well as from architectural design firms and for soil investigation. This is good news. Still unclear is the steps that will be taken to improve education in already existing institutions. In Patna University, a faculty member told me, it is entirely possible for examinations to be delayed by two or three years, and when examinations are finally held, everyone feels free to cheat. A nun who was the proctor at an examination in Patna Women's College was asked by a woman she had caught copying answers from hidden notes: "What kind of a Christian are you? Why are you not showing any compassion? My husband was sick all night. I took care of him." One doesn't need to recall well-worn stories about how Nalanda University's nine-storied library burned for months after being destroyed by invaders in 1197 CE, to point out how impossibly distant the history of a cosmopolitan university founded in the fifth century appears in comparison to the meager reality of present-day Bihar.

But comparisons are invidious. Let us return to the gallery of historical portraits in a schoolboy's notebook. The record began with the leggy and bony dancing girl in bronze from Mohenjo-daro dating to 2,500 BCE. She was naked except for the bangles on her left arm, her right hand resting insouciantly on her jutting hip. Then there was Buddha's transcendental smile. King Kanishka (127–151 CE), whose kingdom spread from Afghanistan to Pataliputra, appeared in the illustration with his squat, broken swords and weird footwear resembling outsized clogs. I recall committing to the page the smooth polish of Ashoka the Great's pillars and the lions mounted on the top, an example of which I had seen in the Vaishali district of Bihar while accompanying my father on an official tour. There was also an image of Samudragupta (335–380 CE) on a gold coin. The great emperor, whose long reign from Pataliputra was one of unprecedented military expansion, sat with one leg folded under him, just as an ordinary day laborer would while waiting on a platform under a *peepul* tree.

Ancient India gave way, after a hundred pages, to medieval India. Now the figures were bearded—a gift to the young artist in the classroom. I didn't know this then, but at the Khuda Bakhsh library in Patna there were brilliantly illustrated manuscripts and books—for example, the *Kitab-ul-Hashaish* from the thirteenth century CE, in which, as the librarian was to tell me many years later, even in the crowded war scenes no two faces are alike. There was also in the same library a priceless book of poems by the Persian poet, Hafiz, given to the Mughal emperor Humayun by the ruler of Iran. In the margins of that book was a notation made by Humayun's grandson, Jahangir, who had opened the book to that page to find an augury during a time of uncertainty in his youth. The words on which his eyes had fallen proclaimed that he would one day become emperor.

The Mughal rulers wore long tunics and turbans, and in a few of those pictures the emperor held a delicate flower in his hand. I drew all these details diligently in my notebook. I had a special affection for the Afghan, Sher Shah Suri, who lay buried in the nearby town of Sasaram. We were taught in school that Sher Shah had built the Grand Trunk Road. He was shown in the textbook with a fierce beard and hazel eyes; he wore a tapering steel helmet with mail descending from it to his shoulders. Did our history teacher tell us that it was Sher Shah who gave Patna the name by which it is known today? No, and it is possible that he didn't know that: the textbook was produced by a national educational agency, and it wasn't designed to pander to local sentiment. Sher Shah's original name was Farid Khan. Under the Mughals he was governor of Bihar, and during that time he once reportedly killed a tiger in a forest with his bare hands. When he became emperor in 1540, he took the name Sher Shah

Suri. In Patna he built a fort and a mosque; the fort, on the banks of the Ganga, has nearly vanished, but the mosque survives to this day.

Ralph Fitch was the first British traveler to visit India, and during a visit to Patna in 1586 he described it as "a very long and great Town" with a flourishing trade in cotton, sugar, and opium.[4] Within a century, the English and Dutch India companies had made Patna an important site for their commercial operations. In the seventeenth and eighteenth centuries other Europeans, like the Portuguese and the Danes, and non-Europeans, including Persians, Central Asians, and Armenians, came to Patna to trade. Cotton textiles, saltpeter, indigo, and opium were among the commodities that made Patna rich.

I didn't learn any of this from my history textbook. The teaching of the history of India had obliterated Bihar. Delhi had swallowed Patna. The Mughal emperor Aurangzeb, who reigned from the middle of the seventeenth century to the beginning of the eighteenth century, made a particular impression on me. In the textbook Aurangzeb was shown with a narrow, concave chest, as if the artist had tried hard to capture his cruel intolerance. Unlike his great forebear, Akbar, who came to Patna to defeat an opponent in battle, Aurangzeb never set foot here. However, at the request of a favored grandson, Muhammad Azim, who was the *subedar* of Patna, he allowed the city's name to be changed to Azimabad. In the opinion of some historians, if the first great phase in the city's history was its role as an "imperial megalopolis" during Mauryan rule, then the second phase, one marked by the spirit of "cultural renaissance," stretched from the city's revival under Sher Shah Suri in the sixteenth century to the rule of Prince Azim in the early eighteenth century. During this period Patna became "a center of Persian learning, Urdu literature, painting, music and other performing arts."[5]

As far as the drawings in my history textbook went, the only competition to the Muslim rulers came, if a bit late, from the Sikh gurus because of their beards and penetrating eyes. The last of the line of Sikh gurus, Guru Gobind Singh, who was born in Patna in 1666, was depicted with a warrior's mien. A trim beard framed a face on which sat a turban with a white plume; at the guru's waist hung a dagger, and on his back was a bow and a quiver full of arrows. More picturesque still, on his shoulder perched a falcon, sleek and keen-eyed. All this was eminently sketchable.

As I try to enter the mind of the schoolboy who connected to the great figures of his hometown's history, I realize that what attracted me most were signs of masculinity such as beards and weaponry, an attempt to cast my own identity in that mold. Coexisting with that impulse of masculinity was the less visible, and not always contradictory, drive toward ascetic renunciation. This might have been due, in part, to the veneration of self-sacrificing saints in a poor land. But I also suspect that my attraction to such figures—and my interest in drawing them—might simply have been the result of guilt induced by an incipient sexuality.

(A small detour. Abhay Mohan Jha, a journalist whom I had known in school in Patna, sent me a document on Patna's antiquity that he and a few others had prepared for the Bihar government. The text unabashedly proclaimed Patna's past greatness. It had annotations like the following one: "In 1663, the Italian traveler Manucci found Patna to be a big town containing many bazaars which were generally thatched. Manucci was in particular impressed by the fine earthen pottery and the cups of clay made in Patna that were finer than glass, lighter than paper and highly scented."[6] This was interesting, but the real story lay elsewhere. After the English edition of the book had been published, the government brought out a Hindi translation. The book had the same title, but this time the names of the contributors and the editor had been replaced by those of senior bureaucrats of the Bihar government's Department of Art, Culture, and Youth.)

Modern India had its own galaxy of iconic figures, but none of them was from Patna. History textbooks included the likenesses of the martyred freedom fighters in India's struggle for independence from Britain. And so did the trucks plying on Patna's roads: gaudily painted portraits of Bhagat Singh, handsome under a hat, or Chandra Shekhar Azad, plump and bare-chested, forever twirling his moustache. In the textbooks, and again on the trucks, there were crude paintings of nationalist leaders: Mahatma Gandhi, bald and bespectacled; Jawaharlal Nehru, with sharp, angular features under his trademark cap and a rose in his buttonhole; and the great Babasaheb Ambedkar, with his outsider status reinforced by showing him dressed in an ill-fitting blue or black Western suit. I didn't try to outline any of them, perhaps because these figures didn't give me much scope for figurative interpretation. Simply put, their faces were familiar to us from photographs and to depict them artistically was beyond any talent I had.

I stopped drawing. That was not surprising; but what is astonishing to me now is that I never asked myself whether or not Patna's past had any artists. When I began work on this book, I read the Patna historian Surendra Gopal's authoritative account of the city in the nineteenth century. He writes about the arrival of painters in Patna after the decline of the Mughals and the Bengal nawabs: these new artists gave rise to the Patna School of Painting or Patna Qalam. Their principal patrons were the Europeans who were in government or in trade; and they focused mostly on portraiture and the depiction of Indian flora and fauna. Gopal's chapter on art and calligraphy in Patna is often celebratory, giving a rich sense of the city's past, but what struck me the most was a melancholy note in the following passage:

In the nineteenth century one of the widespread hobbies of the rich of Patna was to maintain aviaries, where they kept varieties of birds of different gorgeous colors. These artists painted birds, which they saw around, and they also painted rare birds, kept in the aviaries of their patrons. According to the connoisseurs, these birds are "admirably drawn and very delicately painted." However, it has been noted that with rare exceptions there is no foliage, no environment to complete a picture, such as is found in the beautiful bird pictures of Manohar, the master court painter of Akbar and Jahangir.[7]

The environment that was being erased in the bird paintings, the missing Patna—what was it like? In the journal he kept while compiling survey reports on Patna and Gaya during the years 1811–12, the Scottish physician and botanist Francis Buchanan wrote that it was "difficult to imagine a more disgusting place" than the nine-mile-long city.[8] The congested sections of Patna were distinct from the sprawling expanse in which were scattered the homes of the Europeans. The European portion stretched close to the Ganga; this area, called Bankipore, included the court, the office of the tax collector, a customshouse, the office of an opium agent, and a provincial battalion. "The inside of the town is disagreeable and disgusting and the view of it from a distance is mean,"[9] Buchanan wrote. When approaching the city from the river, the view was better, mostly because of the European houses. But also because, as the good doctor noted, the scene was "enlivened by a great number of fine-formed native women that frequent the banks to bring water."[10] This afforded him little consolation because, then as now, what was inescapable was the sight and smell of shit on the banks of the river. Buchanan noted that what the visitor saw when approaching the bank was a steep clay slope devoid of any greenery "and covered with all manner of impurities, for it is the favourite retreat of the votaries of Cloacina, accompanied by the swine and curs that devour the offerings."

I HAVE WRITTEN about myself in these pages as a young aspiring artist. But how is art viewed or collected in Patna? I went to Quila House on the banks of the Ganga because, thumbing through an old copy of *India: The Rough Guide*, which had cost me twenty-five cents in a garage sale in upstate New York, I had made the discovery that Napoleon's four-poster bed was in a museum in Patna.

What was Napoleon's bed doing in Patna? It turned out to be part of the private collection of a local Marwari family. The four-poster wasn't really Napoleon Bonaparte's; instead, it had belonged to Napoleon III, emperor of France from 1852 to 1870. But that wasn't the main disappointment. I'm not sure why a royal personage would have slept on such a bed: it was not very large and appeared, no doubt because of its age, dull and unremarkable. On the wooden canopy and the side rails were small painted scenes. The central painting showed a gentleman and a lady wearing the formal clothes of that era, a mix of pink and blue and yellow, seated outside among trees and flowers. A lamb had been placed peaceably close to them—this was something even I could have drawn. The bed didn't have a mattress, and bits of rotted fabric that might have once served as skirting lay limply on the floor. From the canopy hung dark tattered cloth like a widow's veil forgotten in a theater closet.

The man who had collected these artifacts was a Patna businessman named R. K. Jalan. Born in 1892, he was a merchant who had apparently made his fortune under British rule. His great-grandson, a young man engaged in real estate development in Patna, had such a practiced air of urbanity that it seemed vulgar to dig for details. For his services in the 1914–18 war effort, the British gave R. K. Jalan the title of Dewan Bahadur. He was invited to royal ceremonies. He rented a bungalow in London for six months when he went to attend the Silver Jubilee celebrations of King George V in 1935. During that trip he visited several other countries, including France, where he acquired the sad relic that I stood facing. So far the story

I was being told was of acquired greatness, but then came a detail that spoke to me more of Patna: during the months that he was in London, all the water that the Dewan Bahadur drank was sent to him from India on ships bound for Europe.

This detail had been narrated to me to stake a claim to an aristocratic sense of luxury. But to read it simply as a story about extravagance or style would be a mystification. In that museum dedicated to the exhibition of the Patna merchant's search for cosmopolitanism, here was a detail about the stubborn clinging to a sense of one's purity. I was intrigued by this traditional appeal to the authentic. The truth was that this traditional man, hospitable and good at making money, stuck to his taboos. As his descendant explained to me, he was close to the British, and he was also friends with the local Muslims—but he didn't eat with either. He was a social and pragmatic man who was completely at ease with his prejudices.

R. K. Jalan might have accepted water only from his hometown, but there was no purity of taste in evidence at his museum. A bewildering, even unfathomable, eclecticism was everywhere on display. Silver plates on which Birbal, Emperor Akbar's famous courtier, had dined, and also a Crown Derby dinner set designed for King George III; items of delicate china that had purportedly belonged to Marie Antoinette, and also a large collection of jade from China dating to the Han Dynasty; a broken wooden palanquin with fine ivory inlays that had belonged to Tipu Sultan, and also an ordinary wooden chair that had broken when Prime Minister Nehru stepped on it to get a better view of a clock. And ten thousand other items, or so it appeared, that were spread over several large halls with rain-stained walls and windows that overlooked the brown waters of the Ganges.

What particular imagination drove this collection? In a booklet I was given, I saw a photograph showing a viceroy dining on the silver plates that had belonged to Birbal. During my visit I was told that Nehru had been persuaded to eat from them, too, one prime minister following the example of another half a millennium earlier. The artifacts had performed a function for Jalan. They had flattered power—the past serving the present, as when Birbal's plates were laid out before the viceroy and then, in newly independent India, before Prime Minister Nehru—and they had allowed other visitors to glimpse a bit of the wonder that was the world. It is true that I didn't marvel at, say, the jewelry and cutlery cabinet of King Henry II of France—such acquisitions represented an overzealous attempt on the part of the collector to identify with royalty—but I couldn't deny my surprise at finding items from all over the world in this decaying house in Patna. Had Jalan so assiduously collected meaningless bric-a-brac because it helped him assume the mantle of worldliness? Did he spend a vast fortune on acquiring these objects because he wished to present himself as a citizen of the world? I don't know. Napoleon's bed was the first object I had sought out after my arrival in Patna because its existence there seemed so unusual. I decided I was henceforth going to look for more ordinary things, not least the people who made up Patna.

A s I grew older and found my footing as a writer, I looked for Patna in literature. Early in the twentieth century, E. M. Forster visited Patna and made Bankipore the model for Chandrapore, the fictional town where *A Passage to India* is set. The Marabar Hills, where Dr. Aziz takes Adela Quested on their ill-fated excursion, is based on the Barabar caves, near Rajgir, a few hours away from Patna by road. Indian writing in English hasn't had much reason to journey to my hometown since then, but when a step is made in that direction, I take note (obsessively, hence the page numbers). Patna occurs once in Arundhati Roy's *The God of Small Things* (259). In Anita Desai's *Fasting, Feasting*, the name comes up early (5). In *The Inheritance of Loss*—by her daughter, Kiran Desai—there's a "fellow from Meerut" (217) but, alas, not Patna.[1] There's also a fellow from Meerut in Upamanyu Chatterjee's marvelous *English, August*. No Patna, however. The place is present only in spirit in the pages of Jhumpa Lahiri's *The Namesake*: "Gogol is aware of the dangers involved: his cousins have told him about the bandits that lurk in Bihar, so that his father wears a special garment under his shirt, with hidden pockets to carry cash, and his mother and Sonia remove their gold jewels." Patna has suffered a decline in the last few decades, at least if we go by the evidence offered in fiction. In his epic novel *A Suitable Boy*, writing about an India immediately after independence, Vikram Seth describes his fictitious elderly character, the politician Mahesh Kapoor, as being "pulled towards Patna every second day or so by the momentous events occurring there, events that were likely, in his view, to alter entirely the shape and configuration of the political forces of the country" (816). In the past few years, there has been only one book, Siddharth Chowdhury's gem of a bildungsroman, *Patna Roughcut*, that has put Patna at the heart of its narrative: "Patna in 2004 is an open city, like Sarajevo in 1992, like Baghdad is right now" (129).[2]

In Indian writing in Hindi, the picture is different. Patna has loomed large in the work of older writers like Ramdhari Singh Dinkar, Phanishwar Nath Renu, and Baba Nagarjun. The pleasure of discovering Patna in their writing, or in the writing of younger writers like Shaibal, is that we are presented with a sketch of the city's social space. Let's take as our example "Ath Miss Tapna Katha," a short story by the Hindi writer Arun Prakash.[3] In this story, Patna is called Tapna. When we meet the story's protagonist, an orphan, she is not allowed to ride a bicycle by her guardians. Our heroine's name is Narmada, though her friends call her Nimmo. Because her maternal uncle and aunt expect her to wake up early to serve them tea and feed their children, she sometimes misses the bus that takes her to college. Often she ends up walking the whole way. In Prakash's three-page-long description of Nimmo's walk to her college, we are presented with a large swathe of the political geography of modern-day Patna. The journey to college is three kilometers long and has three stages.

In the first stage, we pass the government quarters. Unemployed youth stand at the *paan* shop, puffing cigarettes in the manner of the film actor Shatrughan Sinha. They aren't thugs; they are the progeny of government employees and, therefore, are well-behaved in a way that borders on cowardice. These youth cast an arrogant eye on Nimmo—fair, thin, and famished looking, wearing an ordinary sari. To them she looks like a schoolteacher at a private school who hasn't received a salary for three months. For her part, Nimmo doesn't look at the boys but at the broken road ahead of her. This isn't a dangerous stretch of the road, but there is always the fear of slipping on cow dung. This has happened twice.

The second stage poses a problem because here one could lose face. The houses that line the road in this stage are the homes of politicians. This stretch of the road is perhaps the most fearsome in Tapna. Fights often break out here, and sometimes there is gunfire. If there is a procession or demonstration afoot, then the city's *goondas* become a part of the local citizenry on this stretch. Armed contractors are to be found wandering around in the area just about any day. The police often offer assistance to them. If a murder has taken place, the police can be expected to take charge and dispose of the body and sprinkle *gangajal* at the site where the incident took place. Innocent folk don't like using this road. But the shortcut to the college passes through here. The problem for Nimmo is that if she walks on the verge she is likely to bump into a *goonda*, and if she walks in the middle of the road, she will almost certainly be crushed to death by some minister's son who is learning to drive. As a result, she walks rapidly and nervously through this stretch. She then reaches the prison compound. The more civil criminals live here; they try to not molest girls in the open. After passing them, Nimmo has at long last cleared all obstacles and reached her college.

Places appear on maps as flat spaces; they don't appear as stories of neighborhoods. The account of Nimmo's journey to her college isn't a flat idea of a place, an empty space colored blue or orange or red. Instead, Nimmo's brief journey is narrated as a brave mini-epic, the writing of an insider who isn't interested in swallowing up the characteristics of a place in one dismissive phrase. How many *mohallas* and how many lives disappear inside one wretched column written by an outsider in the *Daily Telegraph?*

When the writer Trevor Fishlock went to Patna, a local journalist greeted him by saying, "Welcome to hell." A few days later that particular journalist, who had been zealous in his defense of the freedom of the press, was beaten unconscious. I read this story in a piece by Norman Lewis titled "Through the Badlands of Bihar."[4] The account, enjoyable and disturbing, also had something that was at once too familiar and mysterious about it. I recognized the violence but realized that there were no details and certainly no explanation. We could have been reading about a primitive society. It left me with questions, and it also made me wonder how others had written about Patna.

I grew up in Patna, but I'm aware that when I visit it I see it with an outsider's eye. A few years ago a Delhi newspaper was bringing out a travel special and asked me to write a couple of hundred words about Patna as a tourist destination. I wrote that going to Patna for a vacation was rather like going to a bus stop for a martini. During my trips in recent years, I have found myself always susceptible to the clichés about heat and dust—the recitation of familiar woes of the nonresident Indian in the motherland—but a part of me has always believed that a trip to Patna offers a glimpse of the real India. I'm not talking about so-called poverty tourism here, but something quite specific. A 2010 report from the United Nations stated that in India it is easier to have a mobile phone than to have access to a toilet. Well, ladies and gentlemen, come to Patna—you'll see that the rickshaw puller has, tucked into the little pocket of his torn *ganji*, a small phone, while on both sides of the street, as you ride the rickshaw to the market or the train station, arises the distinct aroma of drying urine. The smell follows you even when you are not on land. If you go on a boat ride on the Ganga, the city reveals another side of itself, like a face glimpsed from a different angle. The boat takes you close to the massive concrete expanse of the approximately three mile long bridge across the river. When the boatman turns around and you are on the way back to the ghat, the human scale reasserts itself in the line of buttocks that forms the indelicate horizon.

I'm not alone in offering such assessments. Other Patna residents have said the same, and not only during the past few years of haphazard development. David Boyk, a researcher at the University of California, Berkeley, pointed out to me that people had been complaining about dirty streets in Patna for at least a hundred years. Boyk sent me extracts from Hindi and Urdu papers to prove his point. On 31 May 1906, *Al Punch* reported that *paaikhana*, or excrement, was being thrown from cars at the east end of the park at 10 PM every night. On 6 September 1906, the same paper published a letter that said that the only place to take a leisurely walk was the Mangal Talab—a retreat from the city's narrow, broken streets and bad smells. But even there, beside the pond, there were no benches. And could Patna's embattled citizenry please get lights around the Mangal Talab for an hour or two most days of the week? A sarcastic editorial from the *Pataliputra* of 1 October 1914 observed that bad odors, mosquitoes, and diseases like typhoid had all been granted refuge in Patna by the efforts of the very hospitable local municipality.

It is only proper that the man who founded an organization to build toilets all over India is from Patna. The man's name is Bindeshwar Pathak, and the organization he founded in 1970 is called Sulabh International. Pathak has said in interviews that his aim is to fulfill Gandhi's dream of eradicating an unpleasant custom: Dalit men and women still expected to carry buckets full of shit on their heads won't need to do so if there are enough toilets. The problem is anachronistic, and so perhaps is the solution—but then, so is the problem of caste, and in its context the exorbitant, and utterly outrageous, failures of humanity.

Pathak was in the news again recently when he gave a check for five hundred thousand rupees (a little more than eight thousand dollars in U.S. currency) to a new bride in a village in Madhya Pradesh who walked out of the home of her in-laws saying that she would return only when there was a toilet in the house. Pathak wants other women to follow this example. He remembers that womenfolk in his childhood home in Bihar would have to wait hours to relieve themselves because they needed the cover of darkness to go out into the fields. The women went in groups because there was the danger of snakes. He remembers that his female relatives often suffered from headaches. My own mother tells me when as a new bride she was taken to the ancestral village home, it didn't have a toilet, and a maid needed to accompany her into the field behind the house. When that wasn't possible, she had to make do with an earthen pot that was lined with ash.

The idea behind Sulabh was that the public would pay for the use of the facilities, choosing to use toilets instead of defecating in the open. Does this happen? Since his retirement from government service, my father has been doing volunteer work for Sulabh. He assures me that twelve to fourteen thousand people use the Sulabh toilets daily at Patna's railway station; each day, the Sulabh complex at the railway station generates revenue to the tune of sixty thousand rupees (more than a thousand dollars). This enormous sum comes from a simple three-rupee (five-cent) charge for using the toilet and five rupees for a shower. When my father recited these figures I didn't challenge him by pointing out that there was excrement strewn almost everywhere on Patna's streets. Nor did I cite to him a news report from July 2011 whose very first sentence read: "It will be 2135 by the time Bihar rids itself of the practice of open defecation, according to a government report. Till then millions will have to suffer the indignity of relieving themselves in public due to lack of sanitation facilities."[5] The report's estimate for Patna alone was more optimistic: by the year 2024, everyone would have access to a toilet.

My own observations, and those of other Patna natives, are borne out by foreign observers. Let us turn again to Norman Lewis, who writes in one of his descriptions of Patna that "men defecated idly, without effort or concealment."[6] But it isn't just the shit, it is also the people. Consider William Dalrymple's report from a few years ago on the state of Bihar: "These days Bihar was much more famous for its violence, corruption and endemic caste warfare. Indeed, things were now so bad that the criminals and politicians of the state were said to be virtually interchangeable: No fewer than thirty-three of Bihar's State Assembly MLAs had criminal records and Dular Chand Yadav, who had a hundred cases of dacoity and fifty murder cases pending against him, could also be addressed as the Honorable Member for Barh."[7] Even ugliness only encourages a certain kind of detachment. I especially remember Dalrymple's piece because it offered the somewhat droll observation: "No one has ever called Patna a beautiful city; but revisiting it I found I had forgotten how bad things were."[8]

Journalists aside, what did other visitors to my hometown think of it? For instance, what were Marlon Brando's impressions of Patna when he visited in 1967?

In the novel *Patna Roughcut*, we read about the appearance at Patna's airport of "an athletic looking man with a beautiful face and intensely brooding eyes, a foreigner in a tight T-shirt and khaki shorts." He has a super 8mm movie camera in his hand. The novel's characters who meet the foreigner are surprised when later they watch *The Wild One* at Patna's Pearl Movietone and realize that the man at the airport was the legendary actor from Hollywood. *Patna Roughcut* was written by my friend Siddharth Chowdhury, who told me he had been born in Patna in 1974, too late to have met Brando during his visit seven years earlier.

No one I met in Patna had seen Brando. And then I had an e-mail exchange with someone who had. In 1967 he was a twenty-six-year-old working in Patna. He was American and had grown up in the town of Amenia, New York, only a short distance away from the town where I am writing these words. His name is Larry Holzman, and he now lives in nearby Woodstock.

In 1967 he spent seven months in Patna during the famine, administering a food program for CARE, the American charity, which fed 5.5 million people across the state of Bihar every day. This work stopped only when the monsoons finally arrived, and farmers were able to till their fields and sow crops. Holzman emailed me a black-and-white photograph from his time in Patna. In the picture, we see him standing next to President Zakir Hussain, the presidential goatee pointing authoritatively, but courteously, at the young American's dark half-beard. Hussain is dressed in a cotton *sherwani* and is also wearing his trademark dark glasses; Holzman, his arms at his sides, is wearing a short-sleeved shirt and trousers. An aide holds an umbrella over their heads. The American's eyes are downcast, as if he is regarding the boys and girls who are sitting in a line at his feet. The children are wearing clothes with holes in them and eating from metal plates placed on the ground. A bucket stands nearby. Holzman told me that his organization had been interested ("after things were back to what passed for normal in Bihar") in providing mid-day meals through schools to hungry kids. But officials told him that the people of Bihar were not beggars. They didn't want photographs of children with outstretched plates. In his note to me, Holzman wrote: "I never encountered an undernourished Government of Bihar official, so I guess people took pictures of them rather than of the malnourished children."

Before he went to Patna, Holzman was a Peace Corps teacher in "a little mud and stick village school" in the Liberian rain forest. During his two years in Liberia, Holzman had been in charge of the

CARE feeding program at the school, providing students with milk powder, cornmeal, flour, bulgur wheat, and cooking oil donated by the United States under the PL 480 Program, also called the Food for Peace Program. From Liberia, he went as a CARE employee to Sri Lanka, which was then called Ceylon. When the famine broke out in Bihar, he was chosen to go to Patna. Holzman told me that he is unlikely to ever forget the long lines of hungry people squatting patiently in the dirt under the hot sun. There was another incident that he remembers: a thin boy, wearing only a string around his distended belly, received his ration of milk—the contents of a ladle emptied into a tin can. Instead of drinking the milk, the boy ran over to the tea shop to sell it.

About Brando, Holzman wrote that the local UNICEF representative had received a telegram saying that he was to pick up someone called "Malo Bando" at the Patna airport. The man didn't know who to expect, and when he went to the airport, there was the Hollywood star! The man from UNICEF shared an apartment with Holzman, and Brando slept there for a night. Later in Gaya, in the UNICEF representative's room in the government guesthouse, Brando drank beer and chatted with them. Holzman told me that the actor was very down to earth. He listened and asked intelligent questions. When they were discussing severe malnutrition among children in Bihar, Brando said that he had never experienced anything like this before. He then said that he had several children, but didn't know where they all were.

I RECENTLY READ an interview with the Irish writer Colm Tóibín. Tóibín had told a class he was teaching that "you have to be a terrible monster to write." Everything is material, the writer was saying, even confidences that someone has indiscreetly shared with you. Tóibín's advice to writers was to go ahead and use the story, even if readers were going to identify the person you were writing about. The writer's credo must be: use it because it will make a great story. Tóibín had said, "If you can't do it then writing isn't for you. You've no right to be here. If there is any way I can help you get into law school then I will. Your morality will be more useful in a courtroom."[9] I was on Tóibín's side of the argument. Whether it was the selfishness of art, or just plain individual selfishness, I had often written about my family and friends, telling myself that they wouldn't mind, or, more egregiously, that they would never read what I had written. And not only friends and family—I had done the same to Patna, the city as a whole. I told stories about Patna because they were a part of my shame at having come from nowhere. Although the shame was mixed with nostalgia, because Patna was all I'd ever had, I didn't hold back. It took me time to learn that what I thought of as honesty, the honesty required of a writer, was also a rejection of who I was. "I disliked Patna when I lived there as a boy," one piece began, "but what I remember most clearly is how much I disliked myself."[10] I came to see that I was rejecting my entire past because I was making myself into someone new. It was easier that way.

Such an act of complete rejection, sparing no one, can be life giving. At the very least, it stimulates the senses. It can be harmful, too, of course, but if it doesn't kill you, it leaves you revived. This is because you have nothing more to lose. You are free to speak your mind. For writers like V. S. Naipaul and his younger brother, Shiva, the rejection of India—and, therefore, of their antiquated past, whose burden they had carried in their heads since birth—must have carried such a charge. Their dismissal of India is no ordinary dismissal: it is an act of willful negation, an attempt to find an identity that sheds all its former psychological baggage. I'm telling you all this because Shiva Naipaul had traveled to Patna and described it as "a town without the faintest traces of charm, a sprawling caravanserai of dusty roads and fenny lanes; a junk-heap of peeling, crumbling buildings, of squatter colonies earthed in tracts of mossy mud; a swarming hive of paan-chewing, meager-limbed men."[11] This was from just one contemptuous paragraph—there was much more before and after, bitter observations as plentiful as the bloated corpses he imagined floating in the Ganga. Here was Naipaul calling Bihar "the subcontinent's heart of darkness"; here he was saying that Bihar "defied reason and alienated compassion."[12]

"You want to know if there is *anything* good that can be said about Bihar?" In Patna an editor had asked Shiva Naipaul that question, and he answered it in the following words: "The truthful reply is no. I cannot think of a single good thing to say."[13] One dismal phrase heaped on another. After a while, you have to start laughing because you are witnessing a performance. Hysteria as travel writing: "The disorder, the dirt, the ugliness is overwhelming. How do men manage to live in a place like this? How is it that they do not all go mad?"[14]

Such rejection should have burned away all of my sentimental illusions. But it didn't; not least because I have spoken to a journalist who was Shiva Naipaul's guide during his trip to Bihar. The journalist identified himself as the one who had taken Naipaul to a village where a massacre had taken place. He was mentioned by Naipaul in his piece about Patna. This man, Ashok Singh, was now a journalist in Qatar. When I reached him on the phone, he was in Bihar, on a visit to his village in Sitamarhi. I asked him about Naipaul's description of him on that trip, as a leftist ideologue who emptily talked of revolution and of kulak and serf. Singh responded that he was definitely "pro-poor" and that he had wanted Naipaul to see what he called with great emphasis *the real Bihar*. At that time he had been studying English literature at Patna University, with a special interest in the "grand masters" of the nineteenth-century novel. Singh admitted that he was drawn by "intellectual glamour" but said that he had found Naipaul superficial and lacking in empathy.

The name of the village was Pipra. The name, when I heard it on the phone, stirred a memory. But I needed to check newspaper records to find out what had happened there. In February 1980 a mob of Kurmi landowners had set fire to Dalit homes: fourteen Dalits, including women and children, had been burned to death. Singh told me that more than a year had passed since the massacre by the time Naipaul arrived in Patna. As I listened to Singh talk, I began to get a sense of what he meant by "the real Bihar." This wasn't a Bihar of helpless Dalits; instead, it was a land of upheaval. The countryside was aflame with uprisings. Singh pointed out to me that the reason the Pipra massacre had taken place was because those regarded as untouchable were getting organized. They were demanding minimum wages for their labor in the fields. Communists were active in the area, and Singh had friends in their ranks.

Shiva Naipaul and Singh left Patna soon after breakfast. It rained, and then the sun came out. The day turned hot and humid. The morning's rain had worsened the conditions created by the monsoon. The road to the village had turned to mud. It was decided that the Ambassador in which they were traveling would be left on the highway. The rest of the journey—a few miles—would have to be made on foot. They walked through soft mud, wading through ankle-deep rainwater. The mud was slimy, and at one point Naipaul slipped and nearly fell. He was obese, Singh said to me. Naipaul, after running out of bottled water, was unable to walk any further. He said he was going to faint and sat down by the wayside. There were no houses nearby, only a couple of huts where a villager needed to be persuaded to boil water. In the report that Naipaul wrote there is no mention of any of this; he writes only that he lay down in the shade of a tree and smelled excrement in the air. Singh told me that after this brief rest, Naipaul declared that he would go no further. The trip was aborted. In the car, during their short journey back to Patna, the visitor said accusingly, "I could have died."

There is no more about Singh in Shiva Naipaul's piece, but they had met again the next day. They were going to travel south from Patna to Jamshedpur, a city with steel factories. Naipaul was in a foul mood. Just when the taxi left the outskirts of the city, he broke his silence and said that he felt he was being exploited. Singh asked the driver to stop the car and took his suitcase out of the trunk. Naipaul's mood changed at this sign of protest, and he began to plead. But Singh pointed out that he had been helping Naipaul without being paid; he didn't expect to be abused for sacrificing his time. Singh refused to get back into the car, despite Naipaul's entreaties, and returned to Patna alone.

I had been drawn by Shiva Naipaul's grand rejection. How exact—and exacting—his language! How appealing his descriptions of gloomy hotel rooms! Then came Singh and the double rejection. The Biharis whom Naipaul condemned had rejected him in turn. It wasn't just the rudeness; more unacceptable were Naipaul's crude generalizations. (An example—here was Naipaul offering a Delhi businessman's assessment of the Bihari character: "He had concluded that the Bihari was almost devoid of ambition in the conventional sense. At any rate, ambition was not associated with productive, disciplined labor. Its place was taken by fatuous greed."[15]) I asked Singh to tell me what his experience with Naipaul had meant to him. He said, "We wanted the outside world to know about Bihar. We were offering our services free. We were students, journalists, and activists. Those days we were pro-Left. Shiva Naipaul had a very superficial understanding of India—and about Bihar he didn't know anything at all."

It isn't difficult to be sensible. A travel writer can quite easily avoid broad, misleading generalizations. He or she can also offer insights. As a new graduate student in Syracuse, New York, in the mid-1980s, I found in the library stacks an article about Patna in a copy of *Granta*. The author of the essay was Ian Jack, then the magazine's editor. His piece was titled "Unsteady People," and it began with the following words: "On 6 August last year a launch overturned in the River Ganges near Manihari Ghat, a remote ferry station in the Indian state of Bihar. Many people drowned, though precisely how many will never be known."[16] I had often traveled on that ferry, and the ferry's owner, described in the *Granta* piece as a "steamer tycoon," lived about a mile from my home. Jack had visited his house, and I read the article with great excitement because until then I had not thought of my hometown as a subject for literary writing. I photocopied that article, and over the two decades since I have made innumerable copies of it and often used it in my writing classes.

Part of the reason for my attachment to that piece is no doubt sentimental—the description, in clean prose, of a small, forgotten tragedy that had taken place near Patna. ("He was a small, old man with heart trouble who wore loose Indian clothes and tapped ash from his Gold Flake King Size into an old spittoon." Or these lines, which explained the title: "The resources of transportation are scarce all over India; there is a continual press and scramble for tickets and seats wherever you go. But young Biharis travel on the roofs of trains even when the compartments below are empty and rush listing ferries like a piratical horde.")[17]

The main reason I like the essay, however, and why I have taught it all these years, is that it links what happened in Patna to a tragedy in northern England. Several months after the steamer overturned in Bihar, ninety-five soccer fans were crushed to death in a football stadium in Sheffield. The two events were unconnected, but Jack, watching the news from England while in India, realized that he was responding as if to a distant tragedy. Examining the responses of the people around him, and also his own experience, Jack shows the reader that Patna is also present in England. Stupidity, ineptness, or failure isn't the inheritance only of one place or one people. By the time we come to the end of the essay, Jack has told us that the inanities that were uttered by politicians after the deaths in Sheffield were unlikely to have been spoken in Patna. No one there would have tried to glorify the deaths or offer lame excuses. The article ends with the words: "Whatever their other faults, Biharis are not a self-deluding people."[18]

About ten years ago, during a visit to London, I met Ian Jack. This was in the offices of *Granta*, which he was still editing, and I asked him about his visit to Patna. He had been there several times, and during one visit, he told me, he had nearly died. He had first felt pain in his stomach, and then he began to vomit in his hotel room. He had a burst appendix. Later he would write about this ordeal in an Indian magazine; in that piece, published some years after our meeting, he said he was thankful for the help he had received from journalists and other strangers. There were brief descriptions of life in the hospital. (Once again, the plain, precise prose: "I was in the windowless intensive care ward. Worse than that, I was in the windowless intensive care ward during a power cut, as it hit the Kurji Holy Family Hospital, just as it did the rest of Patna."[19]) When he was out of intensive care, the scene that Jack saw outside was the same one I had witnessed during all my years at the nearby St. Michael's High School, the endless hours spent gazing out of the window as a distraction from whatever was going on inside: "I got a room with a view of the Ganges and watched country boats with their rough brown sails move up and down the river. On the far bank, men towed them against the current with a rope. I watched this living, toiling world with a new respect, and affection." Affection! Respect for half-naked, nameless toiling figures! Where a Shiva Naipaul would only have seized the chance to pour scorn on a civilization that gave evidence of remaining mired in another century, Jack was more empathetic. For the most part, he observed without sentiment or pity. He avoided broad generalizations and humbug. I have not kept count of the times I have asked myself, even while writing these words, whether I have successfully followed his example.

The reason why Jack was in Patna when he was taken to the hospital was purely journalistic: he wanted to find the lawyer who had represented in court "a man who had spent thirty years in jails and lunatic asylums for the crime of being found without a ticket on the Assam Mail." I recently asked Jack if he had been able to find the lawyer. He replied that after his operation at the Kurji Holy Family Hospital, he had gone to London to convalesce. Then he went back to Patna and found the lawyer. More than that, he also found the prisoner that the man had freed. He was a laborer from Nepal, or at least from the Himalayan foothills, and was arrested when he was traveling to a job on a tea plantation in Assam. There had been an argument with the ticket inspector, and the man had drawn a *khukri*. No one was hurt, and the thirty years he subsequently served in prison seemed to have been a result of bureaucratic mismanagement. Jack told me that the former prisoner was living just outside the jail at Kishanganj, looked after by the same man who had been his warder inside: "He said he missed prison life—regular food, a film show once a week."

There are three Patnas. One Patna is made up of the people who were born or grew to adulthood there and then moved away. Their achievements, as well as failures, now perforce reflect on Patna; this group of people is a great contributor to the mythology of Patna, sometimes of the saccharine, Photoshopped variety you encounter on YouTube or random Wikipedia pages. The second Patna is of those who were not able to leave, for one reason or another, and they are the only ones who truly belong there. A few of them have become enormously successful, particularly in business, politics, or education. There is also a third Patna—the city that is the destination of those for whom it is a matter of life and death. These are the people who come to Patna because they see a need in others—I'm talking here of political activists—or because they are themselves in dire need, such as poor students or those requiring urgent medical help. This third Patna doesn't make Patna great, but it gives it intensity; it even makes it meaningful and necessary.

Let me re-create for you the first Patna, the one that exists elsewhere.

Once a student at Patna's art college, Subodh Gupta dazzled the world of art. He sold a painting about migrants—titled *Saat Samun-*

dar Paar, or "Across the Seven Seas"—in an auction at Christie's for $1.2 million. Today we associate Gupta with his signature bright utensils of stainless steel. Even his sculpture for the famous series of Absolut Vodka ads shows the bottle filled with pots and pans. What are steel *bartans* doing in his art? And do they explain to some extent how he got there from here?

Here's a critic writing about Gupta's shiny Absolut sculpture: "This deceptively simple-looking bottle is garbed in the high gloss sheen of the familiar, homely, stainless steel forms, and is a commentary on contemporary India, transitions, and the inherent contradictions of globalization."[1] The marching army of abstractions tramples on concrete histories. Here's a different story that can be told about that Absolut sculpture. In the late 1960s and early 1970s, Gupta was a schoolboy in Khagaul, a town outside Patna, where his father worked as a railway guard. The youngest of Gupta's sisters made a discovery. Companies that manufactured stainless steel utensils had hit on a scheme that turned ordinary consumers into salesmen and saleswomen. If you sold three *thalis*, you would get two for free. Gupta's sister was very successful at persuading friends and neighbors to buy stainless steel ware, and this meant that the family was no longer eating from the dull brass plates they had used till then. Twenty years later, the page turned. Gupta was in his kitchen, cooking, and thinking that his art lacked luster. That's when the stainless steel *thalis* of his childhood swam into view. The steel plates had shine. They could make his installations gleam and give them not only the form they needed, but also the content. Their content was the living link that they established to his childhood.

When Gupta told me this story, we were sitting in his huge concrete-and-glass studio in Gurgaon, eating lunch from stainless steel *thalis*. But the point Gupta was making was that he had found his language, the recognizable idiom of his art, by returning to himself.

Gupta displays an attitude of fearlessness. You think of Marcel Duchamp and his famous *Fountain*. Duchamp's urinal shocked viewers. Like Duchamp, Gupta has brought the mundane into the museum. In this fearlessness, there is also a desire to speak to other, more famous, artists as equals. Delighted by Duchamp's drawing of a moustache on the postcard showing the portrait of Mona Lisa, Gupta went ahead and cast that work as a sculpture in black bronze. When Yves Klein smeared models with blue paint, using women's bodies as living brushes, Gupta's riposte was to produce a series of prints in which he used male genitalia, presumably his own. One of the first works of his that I saw showed the artist lolling on a black leather sofa, naked and covered in Vaseline, looking defiantly at the camera.

Despite the flamboyance of this brand of artistic production, I find more provocative, and moving, Gupta's assertiveness in works like *Saat Samundar Paar*. The scene portrayed is a recognizable one, familiar to anyone who has seen workers returning to India from the Gulf and places farther afield. In the center of the painting is a cardboard carton bound by red nylon rope; on the carton is written with a marker: GANESH DAS DXB TO DELHI. The carton sits on an airport trolley. Above it is a black suitcase with a luggage tag. We cannot see the head of the man who has his hand on the trolley: in this space of transience, this Everyman is represented only by his boxes. A painting like that brings to the gallery space the sudden intimation of migrant lives and difficult labor and sweat.

There are other such examples in Gupta's art. On a seven-foot-wide stainless steel *thali* are strewn the worn *chappals* and sandals of workers. This installation is called *I Believe You*. The owners of that footwear would not have been able to cross borders, and now those objects seem to carry a sense of their loneliness in the cold gallery air. When the fashion company Chanel commissioned him to make a video on bags, Gupta produced *All Things Are Inside*, a documentary work showing Indian migrant workers in Dubai packing their bags. We are no longer looking at fashion accessories; we are offered the interiors of human lives. Even the idea of the bag undergoes a change when we watch a pink print blanket wrapped and then tied by blue nylon before an address label is pasted on it. In another installation called *Everything Is Inside*, bundles cast in metal sit on the sheared top of a black and yellow Ambassador taxi. This is why metal was invented as a sculptural form: not because it can be melted and molded, but because it can give weight and dignity to the fragile bundle that makes up a poor man's life.

While he was studying art in Patna, Gupta learned very little. He wasn't taught any art history. Names like Duchamp were later discoveries. Gupta says that in our teaching in art we are at least forty years behind the rest of the world. He may have learned more by doing theater. One of the people who directed him in plays in Patna, the writer Robin Shaw Pushp, encouraged Gupta to become an artist. Gupta's father had died when he was in the seventh grade; after that he had studied in a village school. But theater filled him with energy. He acted and always drew all the posters. When Pushp's wife wrote a book on domestic science, Gupta did the drawings for her. Pushp told Gupta about the art college in Patna and put him on the path to becoming a professional artist.

To become the artist he is now, Gupta had to leave Patna and then come back to it to tell his story in his own way. In other words, Gupta has had to become assertive about his roots, and he has had to find a language to feed his talent and his imagination. When I stopped by his home a year ago, he told me he was planning a new work, a performance that would involve his feeding five or six priests who ate food to appease the souls of the dead. I knew about these priests from my childhood. They were reputed to have huge appetites. They chanted loudly, wrangled for money, and put away enormous quantities of food. I could see what Gupta was doing.

He was reaching back into the memories of ritual and mourning and making art from their dramatic reenactment. The past was an installation. This has been easy to see in Gupta's art for at least a decade and a half. He has gone back to the land, but he has not done so alone. Cow dung couldn't have been a part of the lives of all his viewers. But when Gupta made a hut out of cow dung cakes in 1997, he was asking his viewers to travel a huge distance and come to his past. As he explained in an interview, Gupta remembered how in his childhood his mother would ask him to fetch cow dung and mango leaves for her morning *puja*. That is why he called this work *My Mother and Me*. When asked about the status of installation art in India, he said that we have been practicing it for millennia. We take a stone, we pour water on it, place a few petals on it, and lo and behold, that stone is God!

In *The Way Home 1*, which dates back to 1996 and which was also possibly the turning point of his career, we see stainless steel plates arranged on the floor, a red lotus in the center—and scattered here and there among the plates are *kattas*, or country-made revolvers, coated in shiny steel. Here art is reclamation. *Haan, hum Bihari hain*. Yes, I am Bihari. That is what the artist seems to be saying, with a memory of the jibes he endured as a student in Delhi. In fact, he is saying it with brilliant flashing lights. In a 1998 work, his self-portrait in acrylic on handmade paper is surrounded by cow dung coated by a transparent resin. Underneath are flashing red LED lights that say in Hindi for good measure, "Bihari."

Let me tell you about another individual who inhabits this elsewhere Patna.

He is from a village in Bihar not far from mine; he grew up in Patna and then, like many others, he came to Delhi for higher studies. His name is Ravish Kumar, and he is one of the best anchors on Indian television. Ravish has a name for our hometown: "Leftover Patna." In the sense in which he uses it, this is the Patna that is imprinted on the minds of those who have left it and gone and settled somewhere else. When they return to the city of their childhood or youth, they treat it like a leftover. As soon as they land at Patna airport, they show how uncomfortable they are in their hometown—such humidity! Such filth! And so on.

Ravish evokes for me the best sensibilities that I associate with Patna. His English isn't very good. However, his command of Hindi, its variety of registers, and even its dialects is impressive. There are a few segments of *Ravish ki Report* that I have watched repeatedly on the Web. I do this because his language—always warm, often cutting, effortlessly poetic, alive with several native species of metaphor—is the closest thing I know to home. I don't think I would have loved him as much if he had spoken and written in English.

One of Ravish's reports for NDTV was called "English Factory."[2] It begins with Ravish's piquant declaration that on those same walls of our nation on which we are used to finding advertisements for curing impotence are now painted slogans for removing another kind of weakness. The report is a tour of the new spoken English coaching institutes in small towns like Meerut. English for Rs 462 only! "You can learn English for so little," Ravish says. "You cannot buy groceries for such a small amount." As the camera quickly climbs the slippery steps on the ladder representing a shining India, Ravish wryly comments in his voice-over about one of the spoken English coaches who promised near-instant expertise: "What the *angrez* [English] couldn't do in two hundred years, he is doing in ninety hours."

The report was a sharp commentary on the pitfalls of upward mobility in India—or, if not pitfalls, then at least its small obsessions and delusions. But what hit home for me was Ravish's disclosure that on his trips back to the village as a schoolboy, he would be given a line in Hindi and asked to translate it into English: "Mere station pahunchne se pehle gaadi platform se jaa chuki thi." I had been tested with that same line when I was a student at a missionary school in Patna. On visits to my village in Champaran, an uncle would present that puzzle for me to translate: "Before I reached the station, the train had left the platform." The question settled as a permanent fact in my mind. I have never lost that fear; the evidence is present in my dreams, in which I'm forever arriving late, unable to board the departing train.

In any case, one of the English-language instructors in "English Factory" tells Ravish that one can never learn a language through translation. The man says, "You have to bring the feelings of English inside you."

As I've noted before, I find Ravish attractive because he doesn't pander to that section of society that thinks and feels in English. In a 2010 report titled "Yeh Jo Bihar Hai" (This is Bihar),[3] Ravish spoke of how there were more roads now. New roads were being built, but he found himself being driven on a road that was still to be built. After a while, Ravish arrived beside a Musahar *toli*, whose inhabitants he described as "the poor sitting under a tree waiting for Gautama Buddha." In Bihar, he said in his voice-over, "60 percent of the people are extremely poor. While they were in front of me, I didn't have the courage to turn my camera on and show the highway to make the claim that Bihar is shining."

We watch Ravish go to a village school near the Musahar *toli*, where we hear that the teacher doesn't show up on time. On camera, the teacher claims that he arrives by ten o'clock. The children protest. One of them, speaking loudly and clearly, says that that is incorrect. She says the teacher isn't being truthful. He had turned up the previous day at one o'clock. Ravish asks the girl her name.

STUDENT: Reena Kumari.

RAVISH: Reena Kumari! You should be the chief minister of Bihar!

The teacher stays silent. Ravish says to him, "Don't hit her later on." Then, in his voice-over, he says: "This is Bihar's real change. Where the system isn't working, people have begun to speak. Even the children are raising their voices."

The camera shows girls on the free bicycles provided by the government: girls on their bicycles, on their way to coaching institutes or college. This is followed by footage of girls in their school uniforms—blue *shalwaar-kameez, dupatta* pinned together at the back—outside the Bankipore Girls High School. More than thirteen hundred thousand girls have received free cycles, and they have changed the face of public space in Patna.

In such reports I find evidence for a story that Ravish once told me about his leaving Patna and arriving in Delhi to study history. His friend in college, Anurag, wrote a twenty-page essay in English. Ravish couldn't do that. He wrote his paper in Hindi, on the Boxer Rebellion in China. The professor, whose name was Anil Sethi, came looking for him in the student hostel. When he found Ravish, Sethi said to the students who were all sitting together, "Iski bhasha se sangeet nikalta hai." A song seems to emerge from his paper. His language sings. "This kind of language," he explained, "comes from someone who has social understanding."

Ravish ki Report suggests to me that Patna is not elsewhere but actually everywhere. Among elite opinion makers, the presence of this search for ordinary things has an enchanting universality about it. I must confess too that I am bewitched by the beauty of my mother tongue, Hindi, as it is used in *Ravish ki Report*—uninhibited, sinuous, and richly figurative. When I watch old clips of the program on Tubaah.com, the language I hear has nothing to do with the inane Sanskritized Hindi used by flight attendants in their announcements when the airplane is about to land in Patna. Instead, it is the language of someone like the legendary Phanishwar Nath Renu, the only difference being that the writer is now walking the street, red microphone in hand.

I HAVE ANOTHER old friend, born in Patna, who now works in Delhi. His name is Sankarshan Thakur, and he calls his move to Delhi when he was fourteen "the grandest thing that happened (in my life)." But this remark needs perspective. I say this because Sankarshan has also written about Patna, with great sympathy: "It is still quite the shabbiest capital we have, but spare a thought for the depths it is having to claw its way up from."[4]

Sankarshan and I met on our first day as undergraduate students in Delhi's Hindu College, more than thirty years ago. I came to know his father, the journalist Janardan Thakur, who never failed to encourage me to write for him. Sankarshan is every inch as much of a dandy as his elegant dad, but there is also a bigger similarity: Janardan Thakur had authored a well-known book on Indira Gandhi's Emergency and the men who were party to that political conspiracy; a few decades later, my friend Sankarshan penned a vivid portrait of the most dramatic politician and fraud of his time, Lalu Prasad Yadav.

When we were in college, I would visit Sankarshan's home in Karol Bagh and find books by Nazim Hikmet, Federico García Lorca, John Updike, Joan Didion, Philip Roth, Ryszard Kapuściński, and Raghubir Singh. The air in my friend's room was thick with tobacco smoke and a cosmopolitan literary identity. Yet the cultivation of a worldly outlook didn't mean he had forgotten Patna, or what it stood for. In his book there are many truths about Patna and the state of which it is the capital. Here is a story that Lalu Prasad Yadav told him: When he was a child living in his village, Phulwaria, Lalu was fond of wearing clean clothes. He would comb his hair neatly. So when he took his buffaloes out to graze, the upper-caste babus would give him a thrashing. They didn't think a low-born Yadav had the right to go about in anything but dirty rags. Lalu now wanted Sankarshan to admire his haircut. He said: "But look, look now, look at my hairstyle, this neat cut, people call it the Sadhana-cut. Isn't it good? And look at the shine on my cheeks. It comes from eating honey from bees that settle on mustard flowers in the winter. Look at my rosy cheeks; this is the color of rebellion against the upper castes."[5]

A few years later, Lalu Prasad Yadav became the first chief minister to be ousted from office on criminal charges—that's true, of course. But what is also undeniable is the history that Sankarshan had recorded in his book. Lalu left Phulwaria when he was six—and came to Patna to study—because of an incident in the village. A landlord passing by had seen the boy writing on a slate with a piece of brick and had delivered an insult. He had said, "This is Kalyug, now even the children of milkmen will learn to read and write! Do you want to make him a barrister?"[6]

The story might well be apocryphal, but what needs repeating is that it is no doubt true for many people in Bihar. For one reason or another, some are forced to leave their villages and come to Patna, and others leave the city in search of something better.

NOT EVERYONE WHO LEAVES Patna to construct a better life necessarily finds fame or fortune; as with most stories of migration, forced or otherwise, for every success there are tens of thousands who fail. But there are also those who find something that cannot be expressed in zero-sum terms of success or failure. There are migrants who have left home in search of the perfect if elusive "balance of *kamai* and *azaadi*"—that is to say, of income and liberty. The writer and journalist Aman Sethi portrays such a man in his book, *A Free Man*.

He is introduced by Sethi thus: "Mohammed Ashraf is a short man, a slight man, a dark man with salt-and-pepper hair; a sharp man, a lithe man, a polite man with a clipped moustache and reddish eyes."[7] When we meet Ashraf in Sethi's book he is a *safediwallah*, a house painter, although he has followed many professions: he had sold eggs, chickens, even lottery tickets, and he has worked as a butcher, a tailor, and an electrician's apprentice. The place where he lives and waits for a contractor to pick him up for a day's labor is the Bara Tooti Chowk, but there was a time when he was a biology student in Patna, learning to dissect rats with what he calls mummy-daddy type children.

As readers we quickly come to see that Ashraf, despite being homeless, inhabits a story that is his self. I saw Ashraf as Patna's ambassador to the streetside court of Sadar Bazaar. More crucially, in Sethi's telling, what we are delivered whole is a living, breathing personality, endowed with an authentic voice that is a gift to the writer. Ashraf's self-description is a vivid, colorful boast: "I'm a mast maula, dilchowda, seenasandook, lowdabandook (A dancing adventurer, with my heart for a treasure chest and my penis for a gun)!"[8] One night, Ashraf calls at one o'clock to tell Sethi that another worker he has met in Bara Tooti is sick. That young man's name is Satish; Sethi takes him to the hospital. Like many other sidewalk *mazdoors*, Satish has contracted tuberculosis. That explains the hollowed-out chest and the moustache caked in blood. A few pages later, when I discovered that Satish had succumbed to his illness, I thought Ashraf was next. But Ashraf didn't die. He only commented about Satish's good luck in getting a send-off at the electric crematorium at Rajghat: "Rajiv Gandhi was cremated there, wasn't he? He must have gone straight up to heaven."[9] When we next see Ashraf, Sethi says that it appears he has upped his drinking again. We get news of demolitions of illegal street constructions by the municipal government. It is dangerous now to do the kind of construction that gives Ashraf and his friends work. Ashraf doesn't want to return to Patna—he can't be a mere *mazdoor* in his own town. Near the book's end, the author has accompanied Ashraf to Kolkata, where he is hoping to find work. A year passes. Sethi travels to Kolkata to see Ashraf. He isn't doing that well; he has been sick, and he needs new tools. Another year passes. Our young author has been away in the United States, studying journalism at Columbia University. When he returns, he finds out about other deaths among those who used to work at Bara Tooti. He also visits Ashraf in a tuberculosis ward in a hospital in Kolkata. Ashraf tells Sethi that when he gets out he would like to sell vegetables.

A couple of days before the last Independence Day, en route to Patna, I met Sethi for dinner at a Delhi restaurant. That evening I learned that Ashraf was dead. Sethi, for a reason I cannot recall now, had been sent the death certificate. I wanted to meet the *mazdoors* in Sadar Bazaar and asked Sethi to take me there. It would have to be early in the morning, he said, while the laborers were waiting for contractors to hire them for work. At the Bara Tooti Chowk, the men sat in a line, waiting. Each had a small bag or wooden box of tools beside him. There were about twenty of them where we first stopped, because Sethi had recognized a friend from the time he was working on his book—a tall, somewhat morose man named Lamboo. To our left, all down the Sadar Thana Road, there was another long line of such workers, men sitting quietly with the implements needed to build walls, carve wood for doors, or give a house a fresh coat of paint. Behind the men, in the area that divided them from the row of still-shuttered shops, were dark puddles strewn with garbage, against which the line of workers presented a picture of neat order.

The Janmasthami festival was being celebrated that day—that explained why the roadside flower stalls were doing well, selling marigold garlands arranged around smaller clumps of red roses—and there was little demand for workers. It had been a bad seven or ten days. The men, nearly all of them from Bihar and Uttar Pradesh, talked of little else. A forty-eight-year-old laborer named Ram Singh, a painter, said: "There's no work, we are dying of hunger." Another man, short and dressed in a blue *shalwaar*, his hair appearing freshly washed, reminded me that Eid was coming up, in a little over a week. His name was Shakeel Ahmad, and he was a carpenter from a village near Moradabad. His main concern was that his children expected him to buy new clothes for the festival, and he had been unable to find any work for a week. How many children did he have? Three. What were their ages? When I was writing his answer down, noting that his youngest, a boy, was only five, Shakeel Ahmad said in an unemotional voice: "The children phone and want money for gifts during Eid. There is pressure on my heart. Will I commit suicide?"

The night we were having dinner together, Sethi had told me that the best advice he got when writing his book was from a friend who asked him why working life was always portrayed as filled with misery. If the lives of workers were so tragic, why didn't they all kill themselves? Where, Sethi's friend had asked, is the joy?

Those questions had struck me that night as the right ones. The answers were present in *A Free Man*, in Ashraf's lively comments on life, his contempt for routine, his lust for freedom. In a system that made use of him and spat him out—often on a daily basis—nearly each of Ashraf's words and gestures seemed a protest against its inhumanity. Not in a look-at-my-clenched-fist-and-listen-to-my-fiery-speech way, but in a thousand different ways, sometimes insouciant, sometimes perverse or reckless. His drinking, his lack of prudence with money, his fights, his witty statements about life and its miserliness were all examples of a wily form of pavement-level rebellion.

I asked the workers about pleasure. A well-built Bihari man, Sunil, who was twenty-eight and a painter, said that he drank every day. What did he like to drink? It wasn't possible to drink a Bagpiper daily—it cost 290 rupees a bottle—but he liked that. And a woman, too, if he could find one. I asked about the expense involved. He laughed. He sometimes got to sleep with a woman for free, and other times he couldn't find anyone for even a thousand rupees.

But the fact was that there wasn't much to feel happy about that morning. Not a single contractor came while I was there. All the coolness of dawn had vanished. It was hot now. Ashraf wasn't at Bara Tooti Chowk; he was never again going to be there. And I was finding it pretty fucking depressing. I was ready to forget the lesson that Sethi said he had learned about the working class and the presence of joy. The truth was that his book had all the movement and voice that the street lacked on the morning of my visit. The book now felt more real. I remembered reading about Ashraf asking Sethi if he was going to make any money from his book. Sethi had already made some money, enough anyway to buy a laptop. When he told him this, Ashraf said, "*Mata ki kasam*, Aman *bhai*, you will make lots of money."[10] As usual, Ashraf was right. *A Free Man* had won prizes in India and was about to be published in the United States. Its young author was well on the road to success.

Ashraf had also said that Kaka would be rich one day. Kaka was the owner of the tea shop in Sadar where Sethi had written that Bara Tooti began its day. That is where we headed now. Tea would be a relief. The shop wasn't a shop: it was a ledge on the side of a shaded alley, with the wall behind it painted a bright blue. Kaka was a large, middle-aged man with a thin moustache. I had imagined him as a rougher presence, in appearance and speech, but he turned out to be soft-spoken and evasive. He stood facing a large pot placed on a glass stove, stirring milk, tea, and sugar. We drank tea and ate the savory that was available that day. We were regarded with some curiosity by the line of workers who sat in the alley with their tea. I didn't go up and ask if any of them was from Patna. Soon, we were ready to leave. Kaka didn't accept any money from us.

I confessed to Sethi on the way back that I had found it difficult to listen to the stories that the men had told me, and in response he said that one cannot write about the poor with one's sensibilities left intact. And yet, he said, he had found that one could not write only out of sympathy and sorrow. I agreed with him but something more needed to be said: out of countless hours spent with Ashraf, Sethi had fashioned an attractive object, an artifact called the book. It was a beautiful thing. I thought of our visit to Sadar Bazaar. One of the pictures I had taken at Bara Tooti was of a man's plastic *chappals*. They had been spotted with tiny drops of paint. A working man's cheap black footwear. The previous day I had visited the artist Subodh Gupta's studio, and I still had in my mind his installation with workers' shoes and sandals displayed on a wide stainless steel plate. The *chappals* I had seen in Bara Tooti would have been a nice addition to Gupta's installation. Art and literature cannot hope to alter the circumstances in which people live; they should endeavor to represent, with as much creativity as possible, the conditions of living. Yet neither the *chappals* that I had photographed, nor anything else written about their wearer, were going to get toys for Shakeel Ahmad's five-year-old in time for Eid. These images and inchoate thoughts stayed with me, and only later did it strike me that I had been nervous at Bara Tooti. It wasn't just the absence of Ashraf. I had questions about the stance of the artist. I was beginning work on this book. I was leaving for Patna soon and unsure about the use to which I would put the stories of the people I met.

ONCE THE WORK had been done in Patna, I returned to Delhi to catch my flight for New York. On my last night, there was a surprise. Thanks to the miracle of Facebook, I had arranged to have dinner with a group of men I was seeing after more than thirty years. We had been to school together in Patna. We were meeting in Gurgaon, at the home of a man with whom I had acted in the school play. I was struck by the luxury that surrounded us. There was a large spread of delicious food and imported liquor. We were waited on by a member of the staff of the Rashtrapati Bhavan, the official home of the president of India. He stood looking into the middle distance, his bearded face revealing no emotion as he listened to grown men reminiscing about things that had happened to them when they were kids. There must have been differences, not least in income, among the people sitting in that room, but they weren't highlighted in any way and I was grateful for that. I was aware of how successful those around me were: bureaucrats, lawyers, leaders in nongovernmental work, entrepreneurs associated with multinational corporations. These were people who had left Patna behind, but Patna had not left them. One man said that he had founded a school for Musahar kids in Patna. The school started in winter and the new students, all extremely poor, were given uniforms and blankets. One of the small boys was having trouble sleeping because he missed the heat of the pig against whose body he would curl up at night. There were several such stories told over numerous drinks. I was surprised by the tales about adventures with sex and drugs when we were in school. I had somehow missed it all. And even now, embarrassed by what I was hearing, I would look up at the face of the waiter behind the bar. How many drunken revelations had he witnessed, probably even in the Rashtrapati Bhavan, with powerful men returning to their boyhood in the stories they told? My friends were unembarrassed, recounting in detail stories about liaisons with maidservants and a neighbor's wife. Stories of drug deals gone wrong. A runaway's account of a trip to Bombay in search of an acting career. Then a friend began telling us about how our Hindi teacher, Mr. Tripathi, had put his hand into my friend's shorts behind the stage where our school play was being performed. Was it the liquor that was taking away the shock? I looked at the laughing faces and then again at the man standing a few feet away from me behind the bar. He was the only one not drinking. His face gave nothing away.

One of my friends said that the majority of those who had been in school with us had left Patna. I asked why. Someone said that it was because of the school that we had attended. He said, "It was like a rocket. It gave us an escape velocity." Had they—we—not left old parents behind, abandoned them in a way? I asked. Everyone else nodded when someone answered: "Our parents are the reason we are here. They pushed us to leave." Then someone said: "We got out because of middle-class insecurity." This was immediately challenged by the statement that the poor also leave Patna in equal numbers. I was told that the number of those migrating out of Patna was fifty times the number migrating into it. Our host said that the young servant he had brought with him from Patna, Raju, had recently left his house to set up a small shop in the same neighborhood in Gurgaon. Raju was enterprising and ambitious, always ready to help my friend out with any requests for food or services. He was earning over seventy thousand rupees a month.

If the first Patna is made up of those who have left it, then the second Patna is those who live there. The first Patna is an elsewhere, and the second is definitely nowhere else. The real lives of the people who live there make up the second Patna. These lives can be ordinary or extraordinary, but what is a given about them is that they are immersed in the practices of everyday Patna, as routine as doing homework or attending class.

Consider Professor Muniba Sami's class at Patna College. Professor Sami had allowed me to attend her lecture on Samuel Beckett's *Waiting for Godot*. I was a few minutes late because I had been lost in contemplation of the cavernous, white-washed building in Gulzarbagh that housed the college; in a previous existence during British rule, it had served as an opium warehouse. Patna was the main site of opium production under the East India Company. Roughly thirteen million pounds of opium were produced annually and sent down to Calcutta by boat on the Ganges to be shipped to China. Sami told her students about the theater of the absurd; that the West lost faith in rationality after the two world wars; about Derrida and the play of the signifier. I counted twenty female students in the class. A male student sat alone in the third row before being joined by a couple of others. Everyone busily took notes, with the avidity of the crammer—I deduced this from the fact that no one was asking questions or making comments on the lecture in any meaningful way. I could see the Ganges from where I was sitting in a back row, on an old wooden bench bolted to the floor. Sami's husband, Shanker Dutt, also teaches in the English Department. He had ordered coffee for me. It arrived midway through the lecture, and then Dutt came up too and sat down next to me with his camera.

When the lecture was over, Sami invited me to talk to the students. I reminded them of what they had just been told about the loss of faith and asked them to write down on a sheet of paper what they themselves were waiting for. Later that night I read their notes, some of them badly misspelled but all apparently sincere: most said that they were waiting for the eradication of corruption, a better education system, and roads. Unlike the characters in Beckett's play, the students seemed full of hope, but it was easy to sense the underlying despair: "My father, an honest officer, is waiting for a time when he can work without pressure from his minister or secretary or registrar or the chief minister." (The next day's Patna edition of *Times of India* reported on my appearance in the classroom. It was now my turn to experience despair: on the same page there was a report about a sixteen-year-old girl in a neighboring district losing her eye after she was shot by an enraged customer at her father's barbershop.)

After the class was over I had lunch with Professors Sami and Dutt. Sami is from an old, distinguished Patna Muslim family. She had met Dutt on stage. Sami told me that she didn't marry till she was in her forties. This was unusual for Patna, but it was partly because she had unusual parents: she felt little or no pressure from her family to marry early. Moreover, she'd led a full and fulfilling life, busy with her teaching and theater acting, and hadn't felt the need to get married. She often went to the movies with her mother.

In Patna's Cine Society, she had watched Kurosawa's *Rashomon* and several of Bergman's films. In September each year, there used to be a three-day festival of one-act plays, and this would fill her life with excitement. The festival has not been held since 1982.

That last detail was yet another indication of Patna's decline. But there was another way of looking at it. Maybe things had improved from where they were only ten years ago. Lalu Prasad Yadav became chief minister in 1990. Even when he was forced out of office in 1997, he kept his hand on the helm by putting his wife, Rabri Devi, in his old seat. During those years, kidnappings at gunpoint featured nearly daily in the news. Goons and their political patrons brandished guns openly, and rifle butts jutted out of the windows of passing SUVs. In 1992 Dutt was sitting in an auditorium at the university, watching a cultural show. There was a loud bang. People shouted that a bomb had gone off. Dutt said to me: "I tasted thunder." Then he saw that there was blood dripping on his trousers. He had a bullet embedded in his wrist.

Our conversation turned to their jobs. I told them that their students, when they had spoken to me, hadn't inspired me with their grasp of language. Sami said that in the past when people like her chose to study English literature, it was because they were good at the language. She said that when you asked students today why they were getting a degree in English, they were likely to reply that they wanted to learn the language. This was a very big difference, and it was disheartening. This didn't mean that these students were better at Hindi, for overall the quality of education had deteriorated greatly. The professors had friends teaching in the Hindi Department, and they constantly complained that their students didn't know Hindi.

Each day that I spent in Patna, I would step out of my parents' house and see posters and flyers for coaching institutes. There were entire streets taken over by hoardings announcing such classes.

Learning in any meaningful sense had been replaced by the culture of cracking the competition code. Here is a small selection of the signs I wrote down in my notebook:

- For Foundation + Target. Akriti Chemistry Classes. East Boring Canal Road.
- Usha Martin Academy. B.Sc. (IT).
- Target Tutorial IIT-JEE AIEEE AIPMT. Com's Chemistry, Pataliputra, Patna.
- ITER Techno-Med (An Ideal Educational Institute).
- Get 95% in Board Marks. Learning Centre for Class 6–12. Helpline no. 09570084267.
- Sikkim Manipal University. Directorate of Distance Education. 15 Specialisation. Affordable Fee. Dual Specialisation. Authorised Learning Centre. NIMATS.
- Organic + Inorganic. Krishna Sir. Office + Classroom. Mob. 9608919381.
- 12th and 11th English Miss Minakshi Singh Contact no. 9334211254.
- IIT-JEE 2012 Result. Guided by: Er. Kumar Anand (IITian) Foundation & Target. Paramount Classes. Mob.: 9304141100.

For me, the explosion of the coaching institute culture was one of the true stories of Patna. It was possible to see in this change the end of education. The pursuit of knowledge, or at least the idea of open-ended inquiry, had been smothered under a nearly industrialized regime of rote learning. But, as is always possible in Patna, a different story also emerges from this mass obsession with beating the competition and finding access to technocratic training. This near-redemptive story that is told about the second Patna has a hero. His name is Anand Kumar.

In the early 1990s, at the age of twenty, Kumar was admitted to

Cambridge University to study mathematics. A handwritten paper on "Mathematical Spectrum" that he had sent to a journal in the United Kingdom had been published. Then the offer of admission came from Cambridge—not to his house, but to a friend's address, where letters were more likely to be delivered. The house in which Kumar lived with his parents was often surrounded by rainwater. Water hyacinths floated up to his front door. Kumar told me he is from a backward caste; his family was very poor. His father worked as a clerk in the postal service, sorting letters in the mail car of a moving train. The family didn't have the money to pay for a Cambridge education, so Kumar sought an appointment to meet the chief minister, Lalu Prasad Yadav, to see if he could get any assistance from the government. The meeting didn't take place, and he came back empty-handed. Of course, he didn't go to Cambridge, but what stayed in Kumar's mind was an insult—a member of Yadav's personal staff said within his hearing, "What has the world come to? Everybody wants to study abroad!"

Today in Patna everyone knows about Anand Kumar. For the past ten years, he has run a program called Super 30, training young students to compete for admission to any one of the branches of the Indian Institutes of Technology (IIT). Kumar selects thirty talented kids from poor families and gives them free board and tuition. Each year his students have been successful in astonishingly large numbers. The first year, eighteen succeeded; the next year, twenty-two; in 2012, twenty-seven. (When the *New York Times* did a story on Anand, it mentioned that the IIT entrance examination is extremely competitive: the IIT acceptance rate is under 2 percent. In contrast, the article said, Harvard accepts 10 percent of its applicants.[1]) What is equally remarkable is that Anand accepts no financial help from businesses or donations of any sort to carry on his mission; the work is sustained by the tuition fees he receives from the hundreds of students who attend his classes in math and science. Anand teaches these classes with a microphone clipped to his shirt, the students gathered in front of him inside a shed with a corrugated roof.

But all this had seemed an unimaginably distant prospect when he was dreaming of studying at Cambridge. When Anand describes the events in his life in the mid-1990s, you are compelled to step back in your mind a few decades—you watch his tale of woe unfold as if in a black-and-white Hindi film, possibly made by Raj Kapoor. About a month before he would have had to make a final decision on attending Cambridge, the family had finished eating dinner when Anand's father appeared to choke. Something was caught in his throat. A medical compounder (the term refers to someone like a nurse practitioner) lived in the neighborhood. Anand ran out to fetch him. It had been raining, and the area around the house was flooded. The compounder said that Anand's father needed oxygen. Anand looked around desperately in the dark and found a wheeled cart that was used to sell vegetables on the street. He placed his father on it and wheeled him to a clinic nearby, but it was too late to save him.

After his father's death, a letter came from the Postal Department offering fifty thousand rupees for Anand's trip to Cambridge. More money would have to be raised, but Anand wasn't interested because his situation had changed. He now had to take responsibility for the whole family—which included a disabled uncle, paralyzed by polio, who lived with them, and Anand's grandmother, who was ailing. The father's death meant that his salary had stopped. There were loans to be paid off. His younger brother, a budding violin player at Benares Hindu University in Varanasi, needed support.

People had suggested to Anand that he could petition to get his father's low-paying job—the application would be entertained on compassionate grounds. But he had another idea. His mother, who had very little education, was enlisted in the scheme. Anand asked his mother to prepare *papads*. Then he put them into packets and sold them door-to-door on his bicycle. He remembers that the residents of Sindhi Colony were particularly kind to him. Each person in that housing area became his customer. The selling of spicy savories gave the family a livelihood, but the future didn't look promising. On the advice of his friends, Anand began teaching math in a room he rented for five hundred rupees a month. At the beginning he charged each pupil only five hundred rupees for a year, but then he increased the fee to fifteen hundred. In two or three years he had five hundred students, then seven hundred. The money allowed him to buy land and build the two-storied house in which we were sitting. While we talked, his mother sat outside on the floor of the verandah, sifting grain and playing with Anand's toddler, Jagat. Anand gestured toward his mother and said that when they got a water connection in the new house, she said that it was the happiest day of her life.

The house that Anand has built isn't in an affluent area. Rickshaws clog the street outside, and many of the houses do not have running water—it's a common sight to see little girls fetching water home in pails. The skeletons of a jeep and several auto-rickshaws sit rusting in the street. The visitor turns from the crowded street into a narrow alley occupied by cows and goats, arriving finally at a large metal gate embedded in a high boundary wall. A tall policeman, armed with a 9mm carbine, is always around. He is provided by the Bihar government. Once a bomb was thrown at the house by competitors who wanted Anand to shut down his teaching center; on another occasion, a gangster, in prison at the time, called and demanded a payment. And once in a suburb of Patna, a man stabbed an associate of Anand's.

Inside the gate, hanging on thin bamboo frames, were gourds on their vines, with bright yellow flowers. Small rose bushes grew in narrow beds. The living room, separate from the house, is where I had most of my meetings with Anand. The room had a sofa covered in orange fabric and several plastic chairs. The only decoration was a plastic carving of Radha and Krishna on the wall. On a desk sat a large computer monitor, a keyboard, and a printer. To one side of the desk was a door leading to a small bathroom, and to the other side was a wooden cot pushed into the corner. Anand would sit in front of me, wearing a *ganji* and a *lungi*, urging me to drink the milky tea that arrived in tiny cups from inside the house.

At Anand's, I met a quiet, soft-spoken young man named Ambit. He was eighteen years old. A few months earlier, in March, his father had died after being knocked down by a speeding motorcycle in Patna's Kankarbagh Colony. Ambit's father had been a telephone mechanic employed by the government. The pension that was due to his survivors was not being paid, and Ambit said that food was scarce at home. He took the test that Anand administers to select his "Super 30." After he passed, Anand told him that he had felt lost after his own father had passed away, and that Ambit should not lose courage. There are many such stories that surround Anand. Another typical story features a youth called Santosh from nearby Bihta, the son of a poor vegetable seller. Even the windows in the school that Santosh attended were stolen. Santosh couldn't remember when he had seen his mother wear a different sari from the one she had on every day. But Santosh passed the IIT entrance examination; he is now doing research in Europe. Anup is another of Anand's successful students. When Anup's eight-year-old sibling asked his mother for rice, his father went out to get food and never returned. These are just a few examples of the kind of students Anand has mentored. His model has been repeated by others, including Bihar's top cop, Abahayanand, who runs the Rahmani 30 in Patna for talented, underprivileged Muslim students in Bihar.

Suffering, struggle, success. These are the familiar themes of feel-good stories, and in this case at least, those themes shouldn't be overlooked. But Anand's genius lies elsewhere. His students come from poor, sometimes rural, families; this is certainly true of the Super 30, but it often also applies to his other students. They don't know much English; they wear the armor of simplicity; on their feet they have *chappals* rather than shoes. Anand has taken such characteristics and modeled them into a character called Bholu. In Anand's lesson plans, Bholu is the Hindi-speaking *mofussil* boy who presents creative solutions to mathematical problems. He also laughs a lot. He is Anand's hero. His antithesis is a character called Ricky, who is arrogant, rides a motorcycle, and—as Anand put it to me—is "suited-booted and speaks meow-meow English." (A lovely, eloquent phrase that—meow-meow English!) Most crucially, Ricky gets stuck in his approaches to problems because his solutions are rigid, rule-bound, even conventional. Through one clever classroom strategy, Anand has not only given legitimacy to his students' pasts and their real, often miserable, circumstances; but he has also succeeded in projecting onto the dominant groups all the social fears that his own students might have nursed in their own hearts. In the minds of the students in the Super 30, it was not they but Ricky who is scared about the IIT entrance examination; they identify instead with Bholu, who has an abundance of answers and is forever full of smiles.

When I look at Anand and his students, I think that is what the promise of Lalu Prasad Yadav's arrival had once been: the rise of the marginalized sections of society and their recognition as leaders everywhere. It didn't happen, at least not for the most wretched in Bihar, and Lalu's own career was fraught and problematic. But Anand's journey has been less erratic. Instead of a tale of broken promises, Anand's educational scheme has raised high the flag of fulfillment. I believe Patna—and the future—belongs to him.

CHAPTER SIX

Emperor of This World

There is also the third Patna. This is the Patna that draws people to it for a variety of reasons, but usually because the region surrounding the city is even more wretched than Patna itself. You can see the inhabitants of this third Patna line up outside the clinics at dawn, sitting on the pavement or on makeshift benches. You find them sleeping on the floor in the hospitals. There are also others who live in this Patna, an even larger group made up of students from *mofussil* towns and villages who are packed into hostels and the rarer and more elusive band, the activists fired by political causes. They have all come to the city because it offers them hope for the future. However, it is the sick and the dying, in Patna in search of health, who provide irrefutable proof that there is life yet in the city, that it is still capable of providing succor.

One evening during my recent visit I found myself at the emergency department of the Patna Medical College and Hospital. I was sitting with the doctors on duty. Someone called for tea. It had rained, and the roads outside were flooded in places. But we were dry inside, the air smelling of medicines and excrement.

Steaming tea was poured from a large, half-black aluminum kettle into tiny thin plastic cups. The tea tasted wonderful. A doctor revealed that the *chaiwalla* put a pinch of Nescafé in the tiny cup and then poured the tea over it. This gave it a kick.

All the beds in the section I was visiting, the cardiology unit, were occupied. The new patients were put on stretchers in the corridor. Temporary pacemakers—gray plastic objects looking like TV remote controls—were attached to their bodies. A man with a limp went up to each of them in turn and took a reading of the patient's heart: a long brown strip of paper emerged from a handheld machine, and he brought it to the doctors, holding the paper as if it were a length of someone's insides.

I must have sat there for an hour. At one point, I noticed that a green curtain had been drawn around the stretcher closest to me. Earlier, I had spoken to the elderly man lying on that stretcher. He was now emptying his bowels. I could hear the sound, and I was terribly impressed by the dignity and equanimity of everyone around the curtain. All his family members, five of them, were standing nearby with quiet, composed faces.

There were three floors above us, all filled with patients. The evening light filtered into the corridors. The patients were having their dinner in bed; in many cases, the attendants were also eating, sitting on the floor beside the bed.

In one room, I was surprised to see three empty beds, and I stepped inside to ask why. On Monday two people had died. The man telling me this was the patient sitting on the first bed. One of the dead was a teacher who had undergone open-heart surgery. The next day another patient had died. Both had died in the operating room, and all the others who hadn't yet been operated on had fled.

This first man had a bandage on his head—why was his head bandaged in a place where all operations were done on the heart?

He unbuttoned his shirt to assure me that his heart had been operated on, and then he said that when he woke up after surgery he had put his hand to his head and found that it was bleeding. A nurse had then bandaged his head.

Did you ask the doctors what had happened?

The man, whose name was Sunil, said, "The doctor told me he was a heart doctor, not a brain doctor."

Back downstairs, I saw the doctor I had spoken to earlier and asked about Sunil. The doctor said that he must have stood up when he was still sedated and fallen down.

Why then had the other doctor said that he wasn't a brain surgeon? My doctor laughed. He told me that the doctor who had operated on Sunil belonged to a scheduled caste.

People from the Left are supposed to object to such statements, but I didn't say anything.

And what would I have said?

I told this story to a friend in Delhi, whose mother is a doctor, and she said that her mother had a more specific complaint. She says that it's all about individuals, but she can't even critique a junior colleague from a scheduled caste or scheduled tribe without having a complaint lodged against her at the Minorities Commission.

Another friend in Delhi, who is from Patna, said that I couldn't simply repeat such allegations. It would be better to ask why doctors take such satisfaction in complaining about their colleagues when really a lot of the blame falls squarely on the hospitals themselves. Look at the conditions! How was it that the patient in Patna was allowed to stand up after a major operation? How could the operating room be run in such a way that he fell and split his skull?

When Sunil was talking to me, there was another man, slight and with a large moustache, who kept him company, assenting and nodding. I asked him why he was there, and he pointed to a boy on another bed. The boy was his son, Suraj. A frail-looking eleven-year-old, he had a hole in his heart. Suraj's father, Mahto, was a day laborer. The surgery had been free, but the expense of staying away from the village, without work, was impossible for Mahto to bear alone. He had collected money in the village, ten thousand rupees, but it was now all gone.

On another floor, a man sitting on a stool next to a patient answered my question in English. This surprised me. He said his name was Ajay; he was twenty-four and was preparing to take the civil service examinations. "I am a poor farmer," he said. The man lying on the hospital bed, staring fixedly at the ceiling, was his uncle. He had been given a pacemaker.

"Are you the first in your family to speak English?"

"Yes."

"Where did you learn to speak the language?"

He said he had been taking classes in the small town of Aurangabad, at a place called Accent Spoken Centre, and he told me that I could find it in the old Malaria Office. His teacher's name was Mr. Monu. There were two hundred students in that class. Ajay earned his living by working as a tutor. What do you teach? "I like English, I try to give him English," he said. Are you married? He smiled bashfully and said, "Her name is Miss Sunita."

The elevator wasn't working, so I walked down the stairs. On a landing an old couple was squatting on the floor—poor people from the village, the man in a dirty kurta and dhoti, the woman in a green cotton sari. The man was caught in a coughing fit. He wanted to stand up and spit in a corner. But his wife, one hand holding a fan and the other rubbing the man's back, said in Bhojpuri, "You can spit right here. I will clean it up."

The loud coughing didn't stop. The old man, who had a wide chest and bare knees, would bend over and then straighten himself in an effort to get up. And his wife kept saying, "Baitthal rahin. Hum dho nu deb, hum dho nu deb." The man was expending almost all his energy coughing but had saved enough strength to grunt at her. Then, success. He was able to clear his lungs. Now he was free to roar at his wife. I reached the bottom of the steps, and his angry voice was still booming. He was the emperor of his world, and he would spit where he wanted.

JAGDISH NARAYAN CHAUBEY, now in his mid-sixties, is a poet and a professor of Hindi literature. He came to Patna from his village, Mor, in 1953 when he was a teenager. Chaubey wanted to go to college. He was the son of a Brahmin priest, and people took him in. In the early years he survived in Patna by teaching schoolchildren Hindi and English. In one home, where he taught in the morning, he would be given breakfast as payment, two *kachoris* and two *jalebis*. At another house, where he taught in the evening, he was allowed to sleep on a cot outside. The streetlight shone on his face and kept him awake at night. Chaubey told me that he had few possessions and was always in dire need; there were many others like him, searching for work as tutors, and he remembers once not having eaten for two days. At the same time, however, he was accepted as a poet in Patna. He was only seventeen or eighteen, but he was regularly invited to recite poems at *kavi sammelans* in the city. He would be on a stage with well-known writers like Harivansh Rai Bachchan and Gopaldas Neeraj. Each evening poets and other writers gathered in a place called the Janta Hotel on Govind Mitra Road, which is now a market for medical supplies. Contemporary giants of Hindi literature like Sachchidananda Vatsayan Ajneya and Sumitranandan Pant visited the hotel, and so did Ramdhari Singh Dinkar and Nagarjun who lived in the city. Anyone who had written a new piece could stand up and recite his work. The local branch of the Communist Party had a publication called *Navjawaan* (Youth), and in its pages Chaubey published poems that he had tried out on his audience at the Janta Hotel.

Today the street outside Chaubey's house, a stone's throw from the Moin-ul-Haq Stadium, is choked with advertisements for classes in organic and inorganic chemistry, mathematics, physics, and biology, as well as the entrance exams for the Indian Institutes of Technology and other institutions. The students attending these classes stay in hostels and homes in the same neighborhood. What goes on at these institutes, Chaubey told me, isn't really teaching or tuition; it is an insubstantial practice called coaching. Three ATMs have been newly installed on that road, and their users are these students who have come to study in Patna. What is disheartening for Chaubey is to imagine the circumstances that have led them to Patna—in many cases, they are the children of rural folk, and their parents have taken the difficult decision to sell their land to fund the children's education. He said that the thousands of students he sees milling around outside his house have "a degraded culture," that they drink and use drugs. These young men, revving their motorcycles outside, sit each afternoon and evening in overcrowded coaching classes. Discussing the advertisements outside his house, Chaubey shook his long face with its gray, closely cropped moustache. He said he had a different relationship to his profession. He remembered every student's name and roll number. Bihar's chief minister, Nitish Kumar, had been his student. The same was true of the deputy chief minister and the chief secretary. They were polite and respectful men, but no one had really served the cause of education in Patna. He said: "In the past twelve years, there has been no appointment in any department in Patna University."

The story that Chaubey was telling me was one that I instantly recognized. I thought of my father, a village youth, who had come alone to Patna for college. On his first night in the city, he had slept on the banks of the Ganges. He spoke fondly of the legendary men and women he had met in Patna: prominent historians, scholars of literature, doctors, scientists, poets, musicians, political leaders, even the first president of independent India. The educational institutions in Patna had declined since then: the tree had been cut at its roots. When he was a young outsider in the city, Chaubey remembered that there was a major literary event each week. There were programs on the radio. The local printers published good literature. When he did well in his college examinations and was awarded a scholarship, he began supporting a poor student from his village who later became a schoolteacher. These days the students who were living in his *mohalla* were simply part of a money-making scheme. His neighbor had rented three stories of his building to students who shared rooms and paid eight thousand rupees for each room. Chaubey pointed at the street beyond his front door and said: "They are swarming outside. They don't look like they deserve education."

Chaubey had presented one side of the picture. There was another side. The students I met in Anand Kumar's Super 30 and the Rahmani Foundation's Rahmani 30 were mostly from small towns all over Bihar. They were the children of peasants or clerks or shopkeepers. The students didn't pay any tuition; their board and lodging was free. Living under a monastic code—no access to television or radio, no newspapers, no cell phones—they labored from early in the morning to late at night. The conditions under which they lived and studied in Patna meant that what the city offered most of all was a community of peers focused on the same goal. One of the Rahmani 30, a young man named Danish Hussain, said that he and his colleagues woke up and went to sleep together. The support they gave each other was crucial to their success: "Teacher se zyada fayda hum ko students se hota hai" (the students gain more from each other than from the teachers).

When I suggested that they were engaging in a more sophisticated kind of rote learning, the students argued passionately that they were doing something quite different. The name they gave it was visualized learning. More convincingly, when they spoke of their studies and goals as members of a minority community, I saw that their aim in life was in no way to simply memorize the right answers to difficult questions. They spoke about the considerable absence of Muslims—especially when one considers their proportion in Bihar's population—in the civil and police administration, in the judiciary, and in political life. The young men were sitting in a circle around me, a large group crammed into a small room with white walls. Mohammed Muez, a young man from nearby Bihar Sharif, was among the last to speak. He said: "In a country where different kinds of people live, if all those who live there do not develop, then the whole country will not develop."

THERE IS ANOTHER GROUP that belongs to the third Patna. This is the group of political activists, leftists of one stripe of another. In the late 1960s and the 1970s, young college students like Arvind Das and Rabindra Ray, who had gone to school in Patna, returned to foment revolution. I was a boy then, and untouched by that history. But starting in the early 1990s, I was witness to the arrival of the activists who were part of a new wave of politics from below. These activists, most of them from the neighboring states of Uttar Pradesh or Bengal or Orissa, were the link between urban centers like Patna and rural sites of peasant revolt like Bhojpur and Jehanabad. These men and women appealed to me because they were unlike so much else in Patna: they were principled; their interest in art and activism was a repudiation of everything philistine in Patna; and instead of manipulating caste politics, as Lalu Prasad Yadav did, they drew attention to the murderous ravages of caste in the countryside. During my visits to Patna I spent a lot of time in the company of these activists. I visited villages outside Patna where small fires of caste and class rebellion had been ignited, and also, on one occasion, a jail where one of them had been imprisoned. Near Ara I went to a village to meet a short-story writer whose arm had been broken by a feudal landlord, and, because of my new friends, I began to read with great interest Hindi writers like Shaibal. All of this might not have changed the society around me, but it had definitely changed me: I was in contact with a Patna that was different from the city in which I had grown up. This other Patna wasn't a dominant force, but it existed at the margins as an omen or a possibility.

Consider Irfan. He was from Allahabad, the son of a highly literate foreman in a cement factory in Mirzapur District. Irfan had come to Patna to do the layout and design work for a left-leaning publication called *Samkaleen Janmat*. Like everyone else from Allahabad, Irfan spoke very good Hindi, and that drew me to him; but he also had another quality, which I envied. He was direct in his speech, so utterly forthright that you thought he was a decisive man, when actually he was only being honest. Unlike the others in his cohort, Irfan didn't primarily discuss politics with me, and this too made him more attractive. He was interested in art. He was very into music. And the reason I'm writing about him, instead of all the other Naxals I knew, is because he was more intriguing. The public and private sides of his life seemed to be held delicately in balance. In him, the life of revolutionary commitment and the life of aesthetic enjoyment existed in equipoise.

In the mid-1990s I heard that Irfan had married a young woman who was a *beedi* worker. This impressed me. I had reached the age when marriage had become a pressing question; each month I fell in love with someone new and worried endlessly about the choice I had to make. A part of me wanted the person I married to fit into my family in Patna; another part of me wanted to do something rebellious. For the most part, I seemed incapable of doing anything. And here was Irfan who had gone ahead and, in a way that was a rebuke to every academic leftist I knew, had actually married a working-class woman!

Irfan now works for television in Delhi. But after my last trip to Patna, I got together with him, and we talked over tea and cigarettes. Irfan told me that the years in Patna had been a gift. He had never wanted to live in an ivory tower, and Patna gave him a chance to live among the people. He thought people were always open there, and it was possible for him to have a real discussion even with strangers. If he had never lived in Patna, he would never have stopped believing in stereotypes. People used to tell him that Patna was the crime capital of India, but he had no experience of crime during those years. The first time he had his pocket picked was at the railway station on the morning he arrived in Delhi from Patna.

I told Irfan that I had waited a long time to ask about his marriage. What lay behind the choice he had made? These are the comments that I noted down during our conversation:

"When the young men in the party began to age, they would marry the daughter of a comrade. The romance with revolution made way for a marriage of convenience. This was a simple routine in Patna. I was scared of that prospect."

"In Allahabad I didn't lack for women. I was a Casanova. Even in second grade, when I first went to school, I loved a girl called Manju. If she didn't come to school, I missed her. When I was older, especially after I had entered eighth grade, girls loved me. In college, in student organizations, it was common to have a lover. There was a Christian girl who came to my hostel. We ate *chaat* together and we went for a walk in the garden. She gave me a ring. She sent me a letter—a barren letter with a rupee note inside—with a declaration of love. We had a relationship and I still search for her."

"In the same way, I search for Anju Shrivastava. She was my Hema Malini. I would squeeze my lips so that I could have the same dent as hers. She didn't respond to me. But yes, I still search for her."

"I met Farzana the same month that Safdar Hashmi was killed. I had stayed at Farzana's home. I wasn't interested in a middle-class girl with her notions of love. I didn't want a *gore-gaal-chikne-baal* type of woman. Mine was not a romantic choice. I had always wanted a big-breasted girl. She had that. She was fleshy. She is ugly to look at, but she is beautiful. Her heart is beautiful. Let me explain. We leave our home and we see two or three auto-rickshaws outside. They are looking at us, hoping to find a fare. To be able to look at them and to be able to see the hope or expectation in the eyes of the drivers, that is Farzana.

"Her father had died, and her mother was deaf. Her grandmother was sick. Farzana was carrying the weight of the whole household. I saw that she wasn't a middle-class girl with subaltern ambitions. I knew such women in the party. I fell in love with Farzana, although we have no support from my family. My brothers have not accepted her. We now have three children."

EVERY BOOK THESE DAYS comes accompanied by a playlist. When I began writing this book I listened to an album called *Jaag Macchhandar* (Wake up, Macchhandar) released by a Patna group, Hirawal. The CD was given to me by Samta Rai, who first came to Patna as young girl, accompanying her father who had been an underground activist in Allahabad. As a child, Samta noticed that when there were secret meetings at her home, her mother hid all the slippers and shoes that visitors had left near the front door in a basket. Even before she was old enough to notice such things, Samta had learned to sing songs about revolution.

Samta is in her thirties now. She is the mother of a little girl and works full time as an activist. Samta performs street plays and organizes an annual festival of plays and documentary films in Patna. On the CD that she gave me, there are eight songs with lyrics by poets like Faiz Ahmad Faiz and Nagarjun. On one of the tracks, the Hirawal singers, with Samta as the female vocalist, sing a poem by

Gajanan Madhav Muktibodh: "O mere adarshwaadi mun, O mere siddhantvaadi mun, Ab tak kyaa kiya, Jeewan kyaa jiya" (O my idealistic mind, O my principled mind, Till now what have you done? What life have you led?). The poem asks more questions, about the loss of pity, the conscience turning to stone, and the choices one makes in life. The music is not melancholy; in fact, it is even jaunty. As I listen to it, I am struck by the fact that I left Patna in search of a life of comfort; as I play the song over and over I am haunted by the zeal and affection of a person who came to Patna and stayed there in the hope of bringing about social change.

CHAPTER SEVEN Emotional *Atyachaar*

I first met Raghav in the early 1990s. This was after I had read his poem "Kavi Nahin Postman Hoon Main" (I'm not a poet, I'm a postman). He lived by the Hindustani Printing Press, near Patna College. Tall, extremely thin, bearded, long-haired, he was modeling himself on the great romantic poet Nirala, I thought. I later heard Raghav repeat a story about Nirala that had also been told about Friedrich Nietzsche after he had gone mad—that one day, seeing a horse being whipped, the poet threw himself on the unlucky beast and, sobbing, asked that the whip fall on him instead.

Nirala or Nietzsche, it really didn't matter. We were sitting in a small, barely furnished room, with the smell of cow dung and urine on the street outside, the honks and the screech of the street interrupting the talk inside, but Raghav would point his fingers to the sky and invoke the names of philosophers like Karl Marx and Nietzsche, Sigmund Freud and Bertrand Russell; poets and artists such as Ernesto Cardenal and Pablo Picasso, William Butler Yeats and Vladimir Mayakovsky, Rabindranath Tagore and Pablo Neruda. Yet he was also utterly rooted in the Indian reality, its beauty and its ugliness, talking at length about the savagery of the massacre of Dalits in nearby Bathani Tola or the flowing fields of Punjab where

Avtar Singh Pash harvested his poems before assassins arrived on a motorcycle with guns in hand.

When I first met Raghav, I was an expatriate returning home and I was very happy to be shown the cosmopolitan Patna that he offered me in his conversation. This Patna dazzled me. When Raghav spoke, I recognized the city described by Jan Myrdal, author of *India Waits* and son of the Nobel laureate, Gunnar Myrdal, who had served as Sweden's ambassador to India: "He who would meet a Diderot or converse with a Voltaire today has a greater chance of doing it in Calcutta or Bombay than in Paris. Not to mention Stockholm! To Patna—but hardly to Stockholm—one might travel to meet a Berzelius. Even if Stockholm has become more hygienic since Egron Lundgren's time, it is still a cultural backwater compared to Patna."[1]

Raghav was then in his early forties. In the wake of the Naxalbari movement, he had written angry poems that had been celebrated as manifestos of revolt. I learned that during the 1970s, when peasant revolts ignited the countryside in Bihar, even during the dark night of Indira's Emergency that extinguished dissent with a heavy hand, Raghav would recite his poems at public readings. His recitations electrified his listeners. Witnesses report that *rickshawallahs* in their *baniyans*, quiet office clerks, restless bands of young students—all these and more went to his readings and were transformed into what radicals call the masses, the politicized crowd, that adoring object that such poetry or art has always fantasized about.

Raghav was a local legend when I met him, no doubt, but he wasn't prolific; in fact, he had yet to publish a collection of his poems. His father had been a prosperous, upper-caste Bhumihar landlord. I learned that Raghav's name wasn't his real one. This name was the one he had adopted in the movement. Also, he wasn't employed. I was given to understand that he was supported by his older brother, a doctor living somewhere in England. In conversation,

Raghav would sometimes let slip that he had been arrested, but he never said where or when or for how long.

After my first meeting with Raghav, when I went back to college in the United States, I translated several of his poems. They were published in magazines and later in a prestigious journal. During my next visit, I took the translations to Raghav and found that he was now a married man. Leela, the daughter of a Communist worker, had fallen in love with him.

Leela was an actress. She performed in street plays and also on stage. She was fairly attractive, with dark skin and a small, pretty face. I found her friendly, ready to smile, wanting to be liked by others. She spoke to me with a great deal of warmth, even familiarity. I felt enough at ease with her to ask—when we were alone, just before I left the apartment that I still thought of as Raghav's—whether she needed any money. She said no.

I saw more of Leela during that visit to Patna. In conversation, she would speak of herself as a journalist and an actress. I felt that she mistook ambition for achievement, and I began to like her less. I should be more honest: I found Leela's artistic pretensions more irritating than Raghav's light-hearted dismissal of her.

A year must have passed, maybe two. Then, when I was in Patna one winter, I learned that Raghav was going to read at a book fair in Gandhi Maidan. I went to the event. Where was Leela? I don't remember seeing her there. Raghav read his famous poem "Kisne Kabhi Poochha Meena Kumari Se?" (Who ever asked Meena Kumari?), about the yearning of young women in love and the pathos of unrequited love in marriage. There were several young men at the back, and they began to snicker and make catcalls when they heard the lines about a solitary girl, in the silence of her room, seeking an imaginary lover.

Raghav stopped reciting. He wanted the hecklers to know that the poem was about the violence that men do to women. He addressed the young men directly, asking them to listen and understand. They fell silent because Raghav displayed great anguish and it was difficult to argue with him. I admired him for speaking up but also for hiding his anger.

We spoke briefly that morning, and then I had to leave. I didn't see Raghav again for nearly fifteen years. But I saw Leela once. In the United States, I received a letter from her, asking if I could help her in her acting career. I didn't think I could, and I didn't reply to the letter. Then I heard that she had been admitted to the National School of Drama, and the next time I was in Delhi, I went to meet her. I had heard that she was having an affair with someone, but Leela didn't reveal anything to me. After our meeting, I walked over to the bookshop in the Shri Ram Centre, a two-minute walk away, and bought the book of poems that Raghav had just published.

Raghav's collection, *History Stops by My Door Each Evening*, contained his famous political poems but also several others that were full of tenderness. These were poems about trees and canvas shoes, bright kites and wet grass. I read the poems, noticed the dates that accompanied them, and tried to stitch together a biography, looking for clues to the life that Raghav and Leela had led in Patna. These poems conjured up in my mind the geography of my hometown: roofs stretching to the horizon, so many lives. Narrow streets, fading sunlight. Mangoes. There was a poem about falling in love during a matinee in an old theater. Here and there in the collection, there was an invocation of life on stage. Was this a tribute to Leela and her work in the theater? Several poems in the collection were recent ones, and I noticed that Raghav had written almost all of them in the year following his marriage. This made me feel happy for him.

In the years that followed I too got married. I asked my father to invite Raghav to the wedding, but he wasn't in Patna. Then I heard that he was sick in Delhi. Someone said he had gone to Mumbai, where Leela was trying to find roles in films. One year I even went to the apartment where I had first met Raghav, but another family was living there. On a winter morning in 2011, a Hindi journalist I met at the Jaipur Literary Festival told me that Raghav and Leela were no longer together. Had Leela made it in the world of films? The journalist told me that a writer we both knew had made a tele-film based on one of his stories, and Leela had been given an important role in it. But the work she'd got was mostly in soap operas. Hadn't I seen her in one? I hadn't.

And then, early in the summer of 2012, a friend sent me a link to an article in Hindi that Leela had written under a new name. A new name to proclaim a new identity. I began to read with skepticism, not least because I distrusted the new name: I felt that it was yet another example of Leela's grand, overdramatic gestures. But the piece was powerful. Just a few paragraphs into the essay, I realized that damp terms like "memoir" or "reminiscence" didn't adequately describe what I was reading—here was painful testimony by someone intent on exposing the truth.

Leela was twenty-three and Raghav forty-five the year they got married. The day of her wedding was a sad one for her. She was uncertain about marrying Raghav. She had written that she couldn't run away because she had moved into his apartment and was always in the company of his sisters, who had arrived for the wedding. After the wedding ceremony, she was exhausted. She returned to the apartment and went to sleep. All through the night she heard her husband talking to a female friend who was a schoolteacher.

A memory came back to me. Had I met the schoolteacher? I had heard about her from Raghav. He called her elder sister. Anu Didi! Was she his lover? That is what Leela called her in the piece I was reading. Anu Didi's birthday was celebrated in Raghav and Leela's apartment. They continued to fight over her presence in their life— once she even urged him to embrace his relationship with Anu Didi openly, saying that if he showed this courage she would support him. Leela was depressed and disheartened; she fled to her parents, but her mother sent her back to Raghav. One day, at Leela's insistence, Raghav agreed to go watch the film *Sardari Begum*. On that occasion, too, they didn't go by themselves. In the theater, Anu Didi sat between the two of them.

I had been in the dark about all of this. The secrets that people and places hold! Clearly, I had got Raghav and Leela wrong. I had not been observant. My sympathies were misplaced. I had offered money to Leela at our first meeting, when she had perhaps needed a different kind of support.

For the first time in many years, I felt an immediate desire to talk to Raghav. I had never forgotten his poetry, but now I wanted to ask questions about other things in his life. The article mentioned that Leela was in Mumbai—I noticed that I was unable to think of her with her new name. She remained Leela in my mind. I imagined her lost in the world of films, among the countless successful and unsuccessful actors in Mumbai, but in my mind's eye I could see Raghav living alone in Patna. I wrote to friends asking for news about him.

A few days later, I had Raghav's phone number. He was in Patna. When I called him, he told me that he had recently seen my parents at a wedding. My father had put his hand on Raghav's shoulder and stood talking to him for a long time. They hadn't seen each other for several years, but Raghav felt he hadn't ever been absent from their lives. This was how Raghav spoke, giving details, naming emotions. He had moved into a new apartment close to where my parents lived. He said his place was very small and would be difficult to find—he said there were "so many shopping complexes" where there had once been fields—but when I was next in Patna we could meet in the park opposite my parents' house. The government had planted trees in the park and built cement pathways. Raghav had been a member of a group that had petitioned the government for this important civic work to be done. *Was he never going to talk about his marriage?* I asked myself while listening to his meandering talk. Then he suddenly mentioned Leela. Raghav didn't ask me if I knew anything about her; he simply assumed that I didn't, and I didn't correct him. He told me that the article she had written was filled with false allegations. It was a conspiracy hatched by a woman, a feminist from Delhi, who had urged Leela to write publicly about their marriage. In fact, said Raghav, the real author of the article wasn't Leela, who was no writer, but the feminist from Delhi.

So far I had only read the first half of Leela's long article. There were specific details that I wanted to ask Raghav about, but that would happen later. The phone call was disappointing. Leela had made serious charges, and Raghav denied them. In Leela's story there was little self-examination or any mention of other men in her life; now, on the phone, I heard Raghav's equally dissatisfying account of a marriage that had been trampled by a woman's ambition and her desire to be loved by many. I asked him if he had seen Leela recently, and he said no. She called him sometimes to tell him if she was going to appear in a new TV series. She had always been depressed and violent, he said, and had in recent years taken to drinking heavily and become fat.

The phone call lasted about an hour and a half. Raghav told me that after Leela's article came out he was frightened by the possibility that he would be jailed for what he called, using the English words, "home violence." But various well-known people, men and women, had supported him. He mentioned the names of a few writers, and then he reminded me that he knew Binayak Sen and Medha Patkar. He had been a supporter of struggles for women's rights. This talk wearied me. I asked him if he had been writing.

"I hadn't written for fourteen years," he said, "but now I'm writing short poems. I have published a cycle of poems recently. They are about love and forgetting."

Following my conversation with him, I sat down and read Leela's article to the end. There were more revelations and, once again, my first response was to believe everything I was reading. In each short paragraph, fresh reports of violence. He had beaten her in front of his relatives. He had turned her mother out of their apartment at night. He had forced her to abort when she became pregnant.

"Main pregnant hoon" (I am pregnant).

"Yeh kaise ho saktahai? Yeh mera baccha nahin hai" (How can this be? This is not my child).

Human unkindness, especially when exhibited among people who were once in love, makes for difficult reading. The soul's sordidness is revealed in its most naked form, behind closed doors. What amazed me about what I was reading was its uninhibited candor. I disliked its sentimentality but wanted to trust its details— when had a woman in middle-class Patna spoken publicly of the conditions under which she and her husband had begun to sleep in separate beds?

There was sordidness in those lines, and they made me feel guilty for wanting to read them, but there was also a certain beauty. Leela had written: "There was a distance of twenty years between the man I had married and myself. In one night of my marriage, I left behind twenty years of my life. I was not able to live those twenty years. Suddenly, I was twenty years older." I read the pain in those lines. I read the repeated phrases and realized that they mirrored—no, mimicked—the lines in Raghav's poem "Who Ever Asked Meena Kumari?" I took comfort from the intimacy of such opposition.

AMONG THE NEW BIG new buildings on Boring Road, there is one with a showroom for Titan watches on its ground floor. That is where Raghav had asked me to wait for him one afternoon last August.

He appeared through the crowd, wearing a maroon silk vest over a *khadi kurta*. In his hand there was a small, stainless-steel flashlight. When we hugged I felt that Raghav had become even thinner. We went for a walk in the park. Overhead, bats were wheeling in the sky. I mentioned Leela's article, and he said that "99 percent" of its claims were untrue. The only thing that was true was that she had had an abortion. But he was blameless. He had been afraid that she would have left the baby on his hands and gone off in search of a career in Delhi.

We sat down on a stone bench in the park. Raghav told me a story about Leela having fallen in love with her Spanish dance teacher—a story Leela denied when I later spoke to her. While we were talking, Raghav's phone rang repeatedly, and each time he told the caller that he would be coming soon. I needed to go to the P&M mall in Pataliputra, and Raghav said he did too—he had never visited it but had heard all the talk about Patna's first and only mall. We both knew the man who built the mall, the filmmaker Prakash Jha. In the early 1990s in Patna I had exhibited my photographs of the poor in America—the exhibition was titled "The Other America," and it was organized by the same activists who had first introduced me to Raghav's work—and Jha was the main speaker at the event. Raghav remembered that he had chaired that session.

During our drive to the mall, however, he wasn't overly burdened by sweet nostalgia. He didn't understand why Prakash Jha engaged in capitalist ventures. He said: "A man who builds malls, what will he really understand of Satyajit Ray or of Akira Kurosawa? It is different when it is a matter of survival. You want to build a home so that you have a roof over your head. But a mall?"

The driver of our car would look up and watch Raghav in the rearview mirror. Raghav never stopped speaking. Patna didn't have roads, he said. Patna's roads didn't have space for common people to walk on. I was listening to Raghav declaim and feeling irritated, but he was right. The local newspaper the next day reported that there had been an accident outside the mall only hours before we got there. A girl and her father had come out of the mall and found a bus bearing down on them. The father pushed the girl out of the way but couldn't save himself. He was dead before anyone could reach him.

I had first visited the mall in Patna a few months earlier. The first thing I noticed were the large, backlit stills from Prakash Jha's films, including my favorite film, *Damul*, and then I saw the fake Christmas decorations outside the glittering stores, styrofoam snow falling down glass fronts everywhere. Van Heusen, World of Titan, Louis Philippe, Wills Lifestyle, United Colors of Benetton, Belmonte, Reid & Taylor. A different world, this, removed from the dark world outside. And who was to say which one was more real or more lasting.

What I found most memorable during that visit was the crowd massed at the mouths of the escalators on each of the five floors. There were no escalators anywhere else in Patna. A ride on the escalator promised a different sort of experience to the people who had come with such excitement to the mall. For the visitors, there was the thrill—and the fear—of stepping on moving plates. But help was at hand—relatives, in some cases a dozen of them, were there to encourage you, push you, or to simply hold your hand. I shared their delight. A couple of generations ago, this was how others must have been introduced to train travel and later, continuing to the present day, the wonders of flight. In the Patna mall that evening, a middle-aged lady was startled when she put her foot on the rising escalator. At first, she tried to leap off. She couldn't. While she was carried up, her black leather slipper bounced down as if by its own will. The shouts and cries attracted onlookers on each floor. The woman was embarrassed and clutched her husband's arm; a younger male, probably the husband's brother, tried to climb down the escalator in the wrong direction. He had to give up after a bit, and he ran to the other side of the mall to use the escalator going down. In the meantime, the sandal kept up its exuberant dance, like a determined performer cheered on by laughing, giggling spectators. I think I took out my notebook and wrote in it that single magic word so beloved of pundits in postcolonial countries: "modernity."

Raghav was initially dazzled by the lights and the crowd inside the mall, but suddenly he went up to a guard and asked: "Is there a shop here where books are sold?" The answer was no. He immediately looked vindicated.

We lingered in the mall for a while longer. During my youth, I'd heard that writers in Patna like Phanishwar Nath Renu would gather at the India Coffee House on Dak Bungalow Road. Later I learned that Raghav also used to go there. Poets recited their new poems; small magazines were born amid empty teacups; reviews were dissected, gossip exchanged, and, in the course of a long night, literary reputations went up in the smoke of Charminar and Wills Navy Cut cigarettes. Places like that no longer existed in Patna. Writers and would-be writers stayed at home and watched TV, unable to afford the faux-chic coffee shops like Café Coffee Day near Regent Cinema, selling pricey cappuccinos and macchiatos. Or they hoped to be invited to workshops and festivals where they would be served tea and snacks. Yet it wasn't only the disappearance of the coffeehouse culture that made Raghav a stranger in the P&M mall; it was also that all his references, his talk of Satyajit Ray and Kurosawa, were dated and irrelevant. The world had moved on. The mall represented the partnership of art and capital in a way that condemned people like Raghav to the absolute margins. He and I were passive witnesses or, at best, sour commentators. Even the youth in their shirts and cheap faded jeans milling around us, waiting to watch *Gangs of Wasseypur II*—youth whom Raghav and his comrades would once have happily dismissed as lumpen—appeared more alive and eager, even relevant, willing participants in a culture that they wanted to claim as theirs. I was suddenly reminded of what a friend had said to me when I revealed that I was interviewing Raghav. My friend is a well-known sociologist in Patna. He called Raghav "an upper-caste Bhumihar poet who had only written two-and-a-half poems." Then he added: "It reveals the cultural poverty of Bihar that you are spending so much time on a small poet like Raghav."

Back in the car, when returning from the P&M mall, we began talking of Leela again. Putting his hand on my arm, Raghav suddenly said something that was at once so simple and incisive that I forgot for a moment the man I was judging and was forced to remember the writer that he was. What he had said about Leela was simply this: "Unnhone ek line kahin nahin likha ki Raghav manushya hai" (She did not anywhere write a line that said Raghav is human).

FROM PATNA I CALLED Leela in Mumbai and asked her if she remembered me. She said yes immediately and then became silent. I told her that I had read her article. She reminded me that I had offered her money, and that though she had needed it she hadn't felt she could accept. She said she had done small jobs, earning five hundred rupees here, eight hundred rupees there, to keep the household going. It was a mistake, she said, that she had been honorable. I made clucking noises, inadequately trying to express sympathy. It was an uncomfortable conversation, not least because Leela reminded me that I hadn't spoken to her in all these years.

People had called her names. She said Raghav himself had often called her a *randi*. She wanted me to ask him why, if he called her a prostitute, did he still write poems asking her to come back? Leela said: "If I find him in front of me, I will slap him twice. I will break his jaw. You call me a *randi*. Okay, accepted. I am a *randi*. But what did you do as a husband? What did you ever earn for me? Did you give me security? Did you give me a child? Did you give honor to my parents?"

It was a stirring performance. I feel small saying this, but I thought I was listening to a woman on stage. Yet I also believed that she had written the article that Raghav had told me someone else had penned. Still, what was most believable in what Leela had said was her anger. Her open outburst, offering a naked assessment, made everything believable. Remember *Rashomon*? It is not until the woodcutter presents his account that we find ourselves face-to-face with the widow as a truly wronged woman. Suddenly, she is no longer pleading for mercy or whimpering for a scrap of love. To her husband who failed to protect her and called her a whore, she says, "If you are my husband, why don't you kill this man? Then you can tell me to kill myself. That's a real man." She turns her attention then to the bandit. She spits at him, saying: "You're not a real man either. When I heard you were Tojamaru, I stopped crying. I was sick of this tiresome daily farce. . . . But you were just as petty as my husband."

Leela said to me that it had needed courage to marry a man double her age. And it hadn't been easy to be single. "You sit surrounded by wolves," she said. Raghav was a "feudal husband" who had always regarded her with suspicion though he was the one having affairs with other women. She said: "Whore? Streetwalker? Yes, I am! Motherfucker." Over the next several days, while driving around Patna, I'd think of what Leela had said to me on the phone. Her anger was so insistent, it stayed with me.

YOU CANNOT GET AWAY from important men in Patna. On street corners and traffic roundabouts, they stand on tall pedestals, solemn men saying not much at all, as if they have *paan* in their mouth and are getting ready to spit. Nearly all of them wear dhotis, and some sport a *khadi* vest. They all wear glasses. The size of the paunch varies. The men often stoop; some have shallow chests, small paunches, sunken cheeks. A decrepit eminence. The only statues of youth are of the seven students from the Quit India Movement who were martyred in August 1942. These tall statues, forming a fluent tableau on a high plinth, were the work of a Bengali artist and were cast in Italy. Young sinewy men, wearing dhotis, holding high the makeshift flags in their hands; one of the youths is bare-chested, showing a powerful chest and muscles—entirely missing in the physiques of the men walking on the street below them. Still, no women. There is a double irony in this. Patna is the capital of a state where many women win elections, but in many cases these women are wives of *bahubalis*, or strongmen, who are facing criminal charges. Even when these women are elected, their victory belongs to others. A recent example is Annu Shukla, a legislator belonging to the party of chief minister Nitish Kumar: she won the seat vacated by her husband, Munna Shukla, who was barred from the election after a murder conviction.

THE PUBLIC SPACE THAT has been open to Leela, and that she has made her own, is the stage. In recent years she has performed in a Hindi dramatization of Stefan Zweig's "Letter from an Unknown Woman."[2] I haven't watched her performance, but in the week after my conversation with Leela, I read Zweig's novella for the first time. The story is in the form of a long, anonymous letter that a distinguished male writer receives from a woman who has long been in love with him. It is an unusual letter, beginning with the words "My boy died yesterday."[3] The woman is pouring out her heart to the famous writer, who has never known her, because she now has no one else left in the world. Ever since she was a little girl living next door to the writer, she has been in love with him. Several pages of the unknown woman's letter described a young girl's erotic awakening through her single-minded attachment to an older writer. I could imagine the earnestness with which Leela would have delivered those lines. Such pain! Such pathos!

The girl grows into a young woman. The famous writer, "with the glance of the born seducer,"[4] mistakes the young woman's willingness to sleep with him. He thinks she is a prostitute. For three nights, they are together. It is through this gentle, even discreet, disclosure that the writer learns that the child who died was his. The letter writer has her reasons for keeping this fact a secret: he would have been suspicious, and she couldn't have borne his distrust. Moreover, she knows that he wouldn't have wanted the burden of being a parent: "I even believe that you would have advised me to rid myself of the coming child."[5] How had Leela performed such lines?

The unknown woman explained that she wasn't accusing the writer. No, she wasn't complaining. For eleven years she had kept her silence and was now unburdening her heart: "Our boy died yesterday, and you never knew him."[6] The letter writer confesses that to give her son a fine education, and to help him grow up among people who belonged to his father's social class, she sold herself to wealthy men. Yet she kept herself pure by not marrying any of her suitors; she wanted to hold on to the illusion that the famous writer would one day want her.

It is now too late. The anonymous woman is going to die soon. Her letter will arrive, without a return address, at the famous writer's door only after she is dead. He will be stirred by the letter, he will be touched by a faint memory, but he will be unable to recall her face.

The novella was a long letter addressed to a famous writer, yes, but it also represented the unknown woman's emergence as a writer. It had been the same with Leela. In writing about her damaged relationship with the poet, she had turned herself into an essayist. Then I had another thought. It seemed to me that the unknown woman had written what was after all a long and intense love letter. Leela had complained to me on the phone that Raghav hadn't come to the theater in Patna when she had performed in the play *Draupadi*. She still wanted his attention, and perhaps also his love. I thought of Leela when I read the unknown woman's plaintive cry: "You have never recognized me, never, never."[7]

Leela performed words that others had written, but in her conversation with me she was bitter about the fate of her own words. No one among Raghav's friends had believed her story. I didn't even mention to her that a young journalist in Patna had asked me, with great sincerity, whether it was really possible to imagine that any man in a town like ours—on his wedding night, no less—would invite his lover to spend the night in his house. The journalist had also disbelieved Leela's claim in her article that once in anger she had poured a pot of boiling water over herself. "Would she not have got burned?" The young man asked.

Later I had the chance to ask Leela these questions, but I didn't, and this was mainly because I didn't think that people can be, or ought to be, left without some secrets. At the end of *Rashomon*, does the viewer grasp what exactly happened in the grove where the samurai was killed? Life is a mystery, and writers can't let its secrets be reduced to a slogan. There! I had found for my vision of Patna my own language of protest: Don't let writing serve as propaganda! This was important because everyone in Patna spoke in the language of protest. It wasn't only Leela, it was also Lalu Prasad Yadav—the man who had ruled Patna for so long, and whose name was linked to one of the most brazen administrative frauds of recent times. Even he would aggressively present his luxuries and extravagances in that familiar idiom of protest.

So I didn't ask Leela any further questions. I didn't talk to Raghav either. The new batch of poems he had given me that last night in Patna included a long poem that ended with a simple thought:

The number of days she spent with me
More days than that have passed
Since she left!

I thought of Raghav and Leela when I came to the end of the poem, but when I reread it, I was reminded of the fact that what the lines said was true also of my life in Patna. The days I had been gone outnumbered the days I had spent there. The pose delighted me, the pose of a poet, studying the moonlight as it fell on the ruins of the past.

Place of Birth / Place of Death

When the bicycle
bell rings twice at the door
I get up in a rush
forgetting that your cycle
is there in a store room
locked up
and it couldn't possibly be you, my son.
The truth strikes me
even before, my head spinning,
I turn the handle of the door.

The summer sun is blinding.
I pray it is the postman who rang
his bell twice. Sometimes, it is.

Your letters come each week.
I am sorry I don't write often.
And when I do
I can only speak
of waiting and loneliness.
These choices, somehow, were never mine.

I wrote this poem and published it under the title "A Mother Writes in Her Letter." I was a student at that time in Minnesota. This poem, on the page I had typed and mailed it, is under a sheet of glass on my mother's desk in Patna. A few years ago, a publisher included it in an anthology for college students in Bihar; students were asked to respond to the questions that followed the poem:

> Memories are sustained through objects/sounds as well. In this poem what is it that reminds the mother of her son?
>
> The poem is also a commentary on the plight of women and their loneliness. Explain with reference to the general status of women in our society.

Ah, the deadening language of academia! The language of understanding instead of the confusion of loss! No, I'm not only talking about the questions asked of the students. I'm critical of my poem's closing line. It comes from an academic understanding of the world: feelings exist so that they can be discussed in terms of their causes and consequences. Personal observations commonly find expression only as political grievances. Every poem must also work as an editorial. My poem sets itself up for responses that ask unsuspecting students to "explain with reference to the general status of women in our society." I will offer no such closing to this book.

For instance.

I went to the Khuda Bakhsh Library to meet its director, the historian Imtiaz Ahmad. I wanted to talk about that period in Patna's history when it was called Azimabad. I had met Imtiaz before. He sent for tea and asked someone to make copies of a couple of articles for me. I wanted to buy a book, and a request was duly made. Imtiaz talked about many things, like the threats that students made these days when caught cheating. He had a theory about the stages of corruption—Patna was now in the third and final stage. There were opinions he had to offer on a string of historians. There was much that was explained, but what I remember best about our meeting was Imtiaz's fortuitous answer to a question that had nagged me ever since I entered his office.

There was a photograph on top of a safe to Imtiaz's right. The young woman in the picture was seated in a studio, wearing a *shalwaar-kameez*. There was something—there is no way to say this delicately—odd about her. Not about her expression, but maybe about her posture or the shape of her head. I'm not on firm ground here and am likely to sound stupid or prejudiced, or both. In any case, I wondered about her. Who was she? But how could I ask? When I was about to leave, I thanked Imtiaz for his kindness. He is a man of such unfailing courtesy that I began to pay him an extravagant compliment. Imtiaz smiled and stopped me. He said that his older daughter, and he gestured at the photograph I had been looking at earlier, had passed away in 1992. She was disabled. One day the family had gone for a drive, to buy Mughlai *parathas* from the stalls near Maurya Lok. When they were coming back, Imtiaz's younger daughter, who might have been three or four years old at that time, said she wanted to visit the small Expo near Gandhi Maidan. Imtiaz told the little girl that they hadn't brought her older sister's wheelchair that day, so he didn't think the visit would be possible. But the child was insistent. The older one then said, "It is okay, Abba. You all go. I will stay in the car with the driver."

But Imtiaz didn't want to do it this way. He said that if they were to go, everyone would go. The older girl wasn't a small child—she was maybe ten or twelve at that time—but Imtiaz carried her in his arms. It was difficult. Imtiaz said that there were many steep steps, and he had long had a heart problem.

When he said this, I thought of my own children and how much I loved them. I might have also thought that I too would have done the same; I don't remember all that I dwelled on in that quick moment. Imtiaz now came to the point of his story, which my compliment had reminded him about.

He said that what he remembers about his daughter that day is her saying into his ear in English, "You are the best papa in the whole world."

How beautiful, I thought. And then I realized that the story wasn't about the love that parents had for all their children, but instead what children offered their parents in return. I was moved by this, and—seeing the tears in my eyes—Imtiaz stopped. Apologizing, he said with characteristic concern: "I didn't mean to hurt you."

"I was touched," I said. "I'm sorry for the loss of your child."

I'm telling you this because Patna for me will always be about parents and children.

PATNA IS WHERE I grew up. Don't people see a city in terms of their own lives—a woman recalling the cinema where she had her first date; the same woman remembering the name of the hospital in the city where her husband died? This thought has taken root in me because I see in Patna's decline, in its pretensions to development, in its plain dullness, the stark story of middle age and death. It's all hopeless, really—that is what Patna and I are saying to each other.

There is a sense I have of Patna that has to do with my youth. With the discovery of sex. It is a bit weird to return to that feeling. Like being at a school reunion, talking about one's teenage crushes or the first awkward encounter with a girl who had been a prized object of collective lust. The real weirdness of my return to Patna is more like an unease: one eye is forever fixed on the past, while the other is turned toward the future. I can recall during a single evening the youthful glories of sex, the distant terror of that yearning, and then be faced with, because I'm in middle age and my parents are in the last years of their lives, the question of mortality.

To return to Patna is to find the challenging thought of death, like the tip of a knife, pressing against my ribs.

In a clip from a BBC documentary available on YouTube, the British historian and traveler Michael Wood steps off a boat on the banks of the Ganges in Patna. In 300 BCE, when the Greeks sent their ambassador Megasthenes to India, he called what is present-day Patna the greatest city in the world. All along the banks of the river, a stretch of nine or ten miles, there were palaces and pleasure gardens. At the time Megasthenes was visiting, Patna was a new imperial city. The sunlight falling on his face, Wood gushes about modern Patna. He speaks of the tangled roots of history, all still alive today. He declares that to walk through Patna is like making one's way through the Indian version of ancient Rome.[1]

I felt pride when I heard that, but I have to admit that my view of history is not so grand. In fact, it is rather narrow and is measured in days. At most months, and seldom years. There is no way to avoid it: when I step on Patna's soil, I only want to see how much older my parents look. Rheumatoid arthritis has seized my mother's limbs, and she finds it impossible even to comb her hair. My father's memory is as sharp as it has always been, certainly better than mine, but the contours of his body have begun to sag. He goes for a walk each morning, but I noticed last time that he was limping. I arrive in Patna and a few days later I leave. Each time I leave, I wonder about the circumstances under which I will need to return.

Introduction

1 E. B. White, *Here Is New York*, introduction by Roger Angell (1949; New York: Little Bookroom, 1999).

2 Ibid., 54.

3 Ibid., 17.

4 Ibid., 22–23.

5 Arvind N. Das, *The Republic of Bihar* (New Delhi: Penguin, 1992), 42.

6 John Berger, *G.* (London: Penguin, 1973), 149.

7 Robert Sullivan, *Rats* (New York: Bloomsbury, 2004).

8 V. S. Naipaul, *Beyond Belief* (New York: Random House, 1998), xi.

9 White, *Here Is New York*, 56.

10 Amitava Kumar, *Nobody Does the Right Thing* (Durham, NC: Duke University Press, 2010), 51.

11 Amitava Kumar, "What Happens in Patna, Stays in Patna?," *New York Times* India Ink blog, 20 August 2012, http://india.blogs.nytimes.com/2012/08/20/what-happens-in-patna-stays-in-patna/.

12 Jeff Ragsdale, David Shields, and Michael Logan, *Jeff, One Lonely Guy* (Las Vegas: Amazon, 2012), 1.

13 Ibid., 17–30.

Chapter 1. The Rat's Guide

1 "Rats! Look who's getting tipsy," Reuters, June 20, 2007. http://www.reuters.com/article/2007/06/20/us-india-rats-idUSL2010477420070620.

2 Mark Jacobson, "Big Scary Ugly Dirty Rats," *New York*, 7 November 2011, 30–33.

3 Phanishwar Nath Renu, *Rinjal Dhanjal* (Delhi: Rajkamal Prakashan, 1977), 29–30.

Chapter 2. Pataliputra

1 K. K. Datta, *Life and Thought of the People of Bihar* (Calcutta: Scientific Book Agency, 1967), 11.

2 Romila Thapar, *A History of India* (New York: Penguin, 1966), 1:75.

3 Fa Hien, *A Record of Buddhistic Kingdoms: Being an Account by the Chinese Monk Fa-hien of His Travels in India and Ceylon (AD 399–414) in Search of the Buddhist Books of Discipline*, translated and annotated with a Corean recension of the Chinese text by James Legge (New York: Dover, 1965), 77n1.

4 Quoted in Surendra Gopal, *Stepping into Modernity: Patna in the Nineteenth Century* (Patna: Khuda Bakhsh O. P. Library, 2008), 2.

5 Imtiaz Ahmad, "Colonial Patna (Azimabad) in some Urdu Writings," *Abhilekh Bihar* (2011), 22–39, especially 22.

6 "Monuments of Bihar," Department of Art, Culture, and Youth, Government of Bihar, Patna (2011), 63.

7 Surendra Gopal, *Stepping into Modernity: Patna in the Nineteenth Century* (Patna: Khuda Bakhsh O. P. Library, 2008), 156.

8 Francis Buchanan, *Journal of Francis Buchanan*, edited by V. H. Jackson (New Delhi: Asian Educational Services, 1989), 178.

9 Ibid., 174.

10 Ibid., 178.

Chapter 3. Patna in the Hole

1 Both Meerut and Patna are towns in the hinterland; they don't find mention in metropolitan fiction. When you leave Delhi by train, you arrive at Meerut in a few hours, and then, if you soldier on, you come to Patna.

2 Arundhati Roy, *The God of Small Things* (New York: Random House, 1997); Anita Desai, *Fasting, Feasting* (New York: Houghton Mifflin, 1999); Kiran Desai, *The Inheritance of Loss* (New York: Atlantic Monthly Press, 2006); Upamanyu Chatterjee, *English, August* (London: Faber and Faber, 1988); Jhumpa Lahiri, *The Namesake* (New York: Houghton Mifflin, 2003);

Vikram Seth, *A Suitable Boy* (New York: HarperPerennial, 1993); Siddharth Chowdhury, *Patna Roughcut* (New Delhi: Picador India, 2005), 129.

3 Arun Prakash, "Ath Miss Tapna Katha," in Arun Prakash, *Swapn Katha* (Delhi: Penguin, 2006), 47–75. See especially 51–52.

4 Norman Lewis, "Through the Badlands of Bihar," in Norman Lewis, *A Goddess in the Stones* (New York: Henry Holt, 1991), 17.

5 "Open Defecation Far from a Closed Chapter in Bihar," Indo-Asian News Service, 25 July 2011.

6 Ibid., 6.

7 William Dalrymple, *The Age of Kali: Indian Travels and Encounters* (New Delhi: Penguin, 1998), 3.

8 Ibid., 16.

9 Nigel Farndale, "Colm Tóibín: you have to be a terrible monster to write," *The Telegraph*, 25 October 2012. Accessed via http://www.telegraph.co.uk /culture/books/booknews/9615673/Colm-Toibin-you-have-to-be-a-terrible -monster-to-write.html.

10 Amitava Kumar, *Bombay-London-New York* (New York: Routledge, 2002), 82.

11 Shiva Naipaul, "A Dying State," in Shiva Naipaul, *Beyond the Dragon's Mouth* (New York: Viking, 1986), 279.

12 Ibid., 267.

13 Ibid., 268.

14 Ibid., 279.

15 Ibid., 269.

16 Ian Jack, "Unsteady People," *Granta* 28 (autumn 1989): 39.

17 Ibid., 41, 43.

18 Ibid., 46.

19 Ian Jack, "Life Flowing on the Ganga, as Seen from My Sick-Bed," *Outlook*, 14 January 2008, http://m.outlookindia.com/story.aspx?sid=4&aid=236441.

Chapter 4. Leftover Patna

1 Uma Nair, "Subodh Gupta: Absolut Vodka," *Times of India Blogs*, 20 February 2011, http://blogs.timesofindia.indiatimes.com/plumage/entry /subodh-gupta-absolut-vodka.

2 "Ravish ki Report" can be accessed at the website www.tubaah.com. The translation from the Hindi is mine unless indicated otherwise. "English Factory" was aired on May 20, 2011.

3 "Yeh Jo Bihar Hai" was aired on August 20, 2010.

4 Sankarshan Thakur, "Why Nitish is the flavour of the season," *The Telegraph* (Kolkata), May 10, 2009. http://www.telegraphindia.com/1090510/jsp /frontpage/story_10943562.jsp

5 Sankarshan Thakur, *Subaltern Saheb* (New Delhi: Picador, 2006), 107.

6 Ibid., 49.

7 Aman Sethi, *A Free Man* (Noida, India: Random House India, 2011), 6.

8 Ibid., 70. The translation is Sethi's.

9 Ibid., 160.

10 Ibid., 80.

Chapter 5. Other Patnas

1 Somini Sengupta, "A Vision of Stars, Grounded in the Dust of Rural India," *New York Times*, 25 June 2005.

Chapter 7. Emotional *Atyachaar*

1 Jan Myrdal, *India Waits* (Chicago: Lake View, 1986), 194.

2 Stefan Zweig, "Letter from an Unknown Woman," in Stefan Zweig, *Selected Stories*, translated by Anthea Bell and Eden Paul and Cedar Paul (London: Pushkin, 2009), 79–120. First published in German in 1922.

3 Ibid.

4 Ibid., 81.

5 Ibid., 106.

6 Ibid., 107.

7 Ibid., 110.

Epilogue: Place of Birth / Place of Death

1 *The Story of India*, presented by Michael Wood, BBC Two. The documentary originally ran on television 24 August–28 September 2007.

Abhiyan Sanskriti Manch (activist group), xiii

Academia, language of, 104

Activism, xiii, 34, 36–37; leftist, 80–83; protestors, 7–8

Ahmad, Imtiaz, as a parent in Patna, 104–6

Ajneya, Sachchidananda Vatsaya, 77

Allahabad, 83

Anurag Kashyap, ix

Ashoka the Great, in textbooks, 16–17

Ashraf, Mohammed, 55–59. See also Sethi, Aman

Auster, Paul, xxii

Beckett, Samuel, xv

Berger, John, xviii

Beur Jail, 1–2

Bihar: Biharis, 41–43, 49, 54, 57; in author's childhood, 12; during Emergency, 86; famine, xii, 36–37; government, 4, 17–18, 20, 22; history of, 16; in literature, 19, 32, 39, 42; open defecation in, 34–36; poetry, 96; poverty, 51–52, 70–71; present-day, 19; "the real Bihar," 39–40; as state, xvii–xviii; students, 78–80, 104; violence, xvii–xviii, 29, 35. See also Patna

Bookstore, secondhand, xi

Boyk, David, 33

Brahmin, xvi

Brando, Marlon, in Patna, xxi–xxii, 35–37

Britain, 21, 26; British rule, 25, 63

Buddha, 15, 19, 51

Buddhist art, 2

Buddhist sites, 7, 18

Cardenal, Ernesto, 85

Caste, 11; play about, xvi; problem of, xvi, 33, 35, 54, 67, 80; rat-eating, 5, 10; scheduled caste, 75; upper caste, 6, 86, 96. See also Musahars

Champaran, 5

Chandragupta I and II, 17–18

Chatterjee, Upamanyu, 29

Chaubey, Jagdish Narayan, 77–79

Chowdhury, Siddharth, 30, 35

Corruption, xvii, xxi, 104

Crime, xvii

Dalits: impoverished, 11; massacre of, 85; workers, 10

Dalrymple, William, 35

Das, Arvind N., xvii–xviii, 80

Delhi: in comparison to Patna, 21, 41, 82; leaving Patna for, 49, 52–53, 93; newspapers, 32; people of, 75, 91; publisher, xi; visiting, xvii, 59, 88
Desai, Anita and Kiran, 29
Didion, Joan, 53
Dinkar, Ramdhari Singh, 30, 77
Duchamp, Marcel, 47–48

Emergency, 86
Emotional atyachaar, ix
Emotional oppression, ix
English: coaching institutes in India, 50–51; Indian writing in 29; people, xxi; spoken, 71; translation, ix
English, August (Chatterjee), 29

Fasting, Feasting (Desai), 29
Fiction, on Patna, xix–xx, 12
Fitch, Ralph, 21
Florida, xxi
Forster, E. M., 29
Freud, Sigmund, 85

G., xviii
Ganges, 26; banks of, 21, 78; boats, 32, 63; in relation to Europe, 24; view of, 64
George V (king), 25
Ghandi, Mahatma, 23
God of Small Things, The, 29
Granta, 41, 43
Gupta, Subodh (artist), 45–47, 59

Here Is New York, xi–xii, xix. See also White, E. B.
Hikmet, Nazim, 53
Hindi, 65, 89; film, ix, 68; Indian writing in, 30–33; literature, xv, 22, 77; spoken, xxi, 50–52, 71, 81; translation, ix; words in, xv
History Stops by My Door Each Evening, 88
Holzman, Larry 36–37. See also Brando, Marlon
Home Products, xix–xx

India Ink, xx
India Waits, 86
Indian People's Theatre Association (IPTA), xv
Inheritance of Loss, The, 29
Irfan: as a political activist, 81; with women, 82–83

Jaag Macchhandar, 83
Jack, Ian, 41–44
Jalan, R. K., 25–26
Jeff, One Lonely Guy, xx–xxi
Jha, Abhay Mohan, 22
Jha, Prakash, 93–94

Kalam, Abdul, xv
Kanishka (king), 19
Kapoor, Mahesh, 30
Kapuscinski, Ryszard, 53
Karnad, Girish, xvi
Khuda Bakhsh library, 20
Kidnappings, xvii
Kumar, Anand, redemptive story, 66–71
Kumar, Ravish (Hindi news anchor), 49–52

Lahiri, Jhumpa, 29
Leela: as actress, 87–89, 98–100; article, 89–92, 96–97
"Leftover Patna," 49. See also Kumar, Ravish
"Letters from an Unknown Woman," 98–100
Lewis, Normal, 35
Lorca, Federico Garcia, 53
Low-born, xvi. See also Caste

Marx, Karl, 85
Maurya, Chandragupta: Mauryan rule, 21; in textbooks, 16–18
Mayakovsky, Vladimir, 85
Megasthenes, 16
Mofussil, 71, 73
Muslim: people in public positions in Bihar, 80; rulers, 21; students, 70

Musahars, 5–8, 10; schools, 51, 60
Myrdal, Jan, 86

Nagarjun, Baba, 20
Naipaul, Shiva, 38–41, 43
Naipaul, V. S., 38
Nalanda, 18
Namesake, The, 29
Nandy, Ashis, xvii–xviii
Napoleon II, 25, 27
Nehru: painting of, 23; as prime minister,
    26–27; treatise by, xiii
Neruda, Pablo, 85
New York: in fiction, xix; flight from, 59;
    rats in, xviii, 2–3; in relation to Patna,
    xi–xiii; upstate, xxii, 3, 25, 36; writers,
    xx
New York (magazine), 2–3
New York Times, xx–xxii, 67
Nietzsche, Friedrich, 85
Nirala, 85
Non-fiction, 12, 18; unlike fiction, ix;
    imagination, xix; ordinary, xiii

Opium, xiv, xx, 63
Ordinary, xiii, xvii, xix

P&M mall, 93–96
Pant, Sumitranandan, 77
Parents, 103–7
A Passage to India, 29
Pataliputra: P&M mall, 93; Pataliputra pa-
    per, 33; under reign of Chandragupta II,
    18–19; under reign of Samudragupta,
    20; in textbook, 15–16; tutorial craze,
    66
Patna, xiii, xiv, xvi; artifacts, 23–27; as
    author's hometown, xi, 106–7; heat in,
    xii, xiv, 32; history, 15–18, 20–25, 104;
    Junction, 1; in literature, 29–32, 35, 38,
    42–43; Medical College and Hospital,
    73–76; museums in, 2, 25; and New
    York, xi, xxii; parents, 103–7; Patna
    University, xiv, xv, 1, 19, 39, 78; people

of, xxii, 6–7, 45–84; rats, xviii, 1–5,
    12–13; stories about, x–xii, xvii–xix, xxi,
    12, 104; theater, xiv, xvi; toilets, 32–35;
    tourism in, xiii, 32
Patna Roughcut, 30, 35
Phuldeo, 9
Picasso, Pablo, 85
Postcolonial, vis-à-vis nation, xix
Postcolonial theory, xviii
Prakash, Vijoy: administrator, 7; rat meat,
    4–5
Proletarian Nights, xiv

Raghav, 92–98; as poet, 85–88, 91,
    100–101; with Leela, 87–89, 90–92.
    See also Leela
Raghopur, xiv
Ragsdale, Jeff, xx–xxi
Rai, Samta, 84
Rakt-Kalyan, xvi
Ranciere, Jacques, xiv
Rashomon, x, 65, 97, 100
Rats: in New York, xviii, 2–3; in Patna,
    xviii, 1–5, 12–13. See also New York;
    Patna
Ravish ki Report, 50, 52
Ray, Rabindra, 80
Renu, Phanishwar Nath, 30, 95
Roads: as connection, ix; in Patna, 23;
    traffic, 7, 11
Roth, Philip, 53
Roy, Arundhati, 29
Russell, Bertrand, 85

Sami, Professor Muniba, 63–65
Samkaleen Janmat, 81
Scavenger, xvi
September 11, xi, xix. See also White, E. B.
Seth, Vikram, 30
Sethi, Aman, 54–59
Sex, xvii, 106–7
Sher Shah Suri, 20–21
Shields, David, xx–xxi

Singh, Ashok, 39–41. *See also* Naipaul, Shiva
Singh, Raghubir, 53
Sinhasan, 8–11
A Suitable Boy, 30
Super 30, 67–71. *See also* Kumar, Anand
Sulabh International, 33–34

Tagore, Rabindranath, 85
Thakur, Sankarshan, 53
Thali, 46–47. *See also* Gupta, Subodh
Toibin, Colm, 37–38
Tourism, xiii, 32. *See also* Patna

Updike, John, 53

Vernacular, ix

Waiting for Godot, xv
White, E. B., xi, xix. See also *Here Is New York*; September 11
Writing, xix, xxi, 15, 29–30, 37–38, 95; mantra, xii; publication of, in U.S. and India, xxii; travel, xviii, 29, 32

Yadav, Lalu Prasad, xvi; in Beur Jail, 1; as chief minister, 65, 80; promise of greatness, 71; staff of, 67; story of childhood, 53–54
Yakshi, Didarganj, 2
Yeats, William Butler, 85

Zweig, Stefan, 98